Elements of Multinational Strategy

Keith Head

Elements of Multinational Strategy

With 23 Figures and 23 Tables

 Springer

Professor Keith Head
Sauder School of Business
University of British Columbia
2053 Main Mall
Vancouver, B.C. V6T 1Z2
Canada
Keith.Head@sauder.ubc.ca

Library of Congress Control Number: 2007933409

ISBN 978-3-540-74438-2   Springer Berlin Heidelberg New York

Springer is a part of Springer Science+Business Media

springer.com

© Springer-Verlag Berlin Heidelberg 2008

Production: LE-TEX Jelonek, Schmidt & Vöckler GbR, Leipzig
Cover-design: WMX Design GmbH, Heidelberg

SPIN 12112463   134/3180YL - 5 4 3 2 1 0   Printed on acid-free paper

To Alice (*obrigado mamãe!*) and Amy (SILWYAI)

Preface

Three events led to the writing of this book. In 1976, my father's employer, Exxon, reassigned him from headquarters in Houston to spend 18 months at Esso Brasileira, in Rio de Janeiro. During the six years we ended up spending there, my father would often talk about issues facing multinational corporations in developing countries and I would occasionally listen. In 1984, I took the Swarthmore College seminar on microeconomic theory offered by Bernie Saffran. I became so excited about the use of economic analysis to explain how the world works that I decided to do a Ph.D. in the field. In 1992, teaching "International Business Management" for the first time, I found a subject with a plethora of interesting questions but very little in the way of a conceptual framework. I began, working together with John Ries, to figure out how to use economic reasoning and data analysis to answer these questions. The result is this textbook.

My goal in writing this book has been to integrate the academic study of international trade and foreign direct investment—the work I do when I'm not teaching—with the actual strategic and operational decisions of exporters and multinational enterprises. The textbooks currently available often have a chapter on trade theory and then another on manufacturing locations, a chapter on foreign direct investment and a chapter on multinational strategies. Thus, the economics and the management are both there but they sleep in separate bedrooms. This is not only repetitive but it gives the impression that management decisions are not directly linked to economic analysis. My hope is to marry managerial decision making in the internationally oriented firm with the conceptual tools provided by international economics.

Additional materials

Powerpoint or PDF presentations are available for each chapter on the website, http://strategy.sauder.ubc.ca/head/book. These presentations contain a number of colour pictures that could not be included in the textbook for cost reasons. The website also provides sample exam questions.

Acknowledgements

My coauthor, John Ries, contributed in one way or another to every chapter. In addition to countless discussions of the facts and theories developed in this book, he has constructively criticized earlier drafts. Chapters 12 and 13 benefited considerably from the inputs of my former student Don Wagner, now at the University of Prince Edward Island. My current graduate student, Ran Jing, helped me revise and augment chapter 9. Discussions with Larry Wosk about his business experiences helped me shape the transaction cost time-line in chapter 4.

I would also like to thank many undergraduate students over the years for finding errors both small and large: James Kondopulos and Angeline Leong-Sit (2000); Kai Hui, Austin Mok, and John Ng (2001); Emily Thorner (2002); Margaret Lung, Greg Perih, and Aaron Adkins (2003); Surina Sproul, Benjamin Rameau, Mandy Tam, Evan Campbell, Vivian Feng, Tara Amiri-Khaledi, Sarah Mertin, Noah Carter, Andrew Shankie, Jina Kim, and Cedric Wong (2004); Jocelyn Tan, Eric Widjaja, and Tammy Yoon (2006); Emma Carswell-Engle, Alice Chan, Bernadette Cheung, Judy Feng, Katerina Goncharuk, Irene Han, Polina Konstantinova, Jill MacDonald, Bobby Movassaghi, Farnaz Rameshni, David Suozzi, Leo Tam, Eric Tang, Jean Whitaker, and Ruo Xu (2007).

Vancouver   *Keith Head*
                                                                  August 2007

Contents

1

Business Across Borders

Think about the day of a typical student in Europe or North America. She[1] puts on a pair of Nikes and spreads some Nutella on her toast. Her Corolla provides economical transportation to school. She downs a Big Mac at lunch with the help of a Diet Coke (or a Coke Light if she's in Europe) while text-messaging on her Nokia cell-phone. Her day is only half over, but multinational corporations have already clothed, transported, fed, and transmitted her.[2]

Firms doing business abroad face extra challenges that do not trouble their counterparts who confine their business within national borders. These firms also have the opportunity to make much higher profits. It is hard to think of any large, successful corporation that is *not* a multinational. This book will analyze the key decisions made by multinational enterprises: chiefly, where to make what and how to manage far-flung operations. First, however, we need to learn the terminology used to describe international business. In this chapter we define the types of international transactions and entities. We then take up the question about what exactly makes international business truly different. We enumerate the six forms of separation that create challenges and opportunities for business that crosses borders.

1.1 Overview of International Business

International business consists of a number of different types of transactions between entities from different countries. The organization in

---

[1] Females outnumber males in the universities of most English speaking countries.
[2] The companies are, in order the listed above, Nike (USA), Ferrero (Italy), Toyota (Japan), McDonalds (USA), Coca-Cola (USA), and Nokia (Finland).

charge of measuring international transactions in a systematic way is
the International Monetary Fund (IMF). It summarizes all international transactions between what it calls "institutional units" (households and firms) in the *Balance of Payments* (BoP). Although we are
only interested in a subset of these transactions, the BoP framework is
a useful way of organizing ideas. For the IMF, transactions are "changes
in economic relationships." *International business comprises exchange
transactions in which at least one of the parties is a firm.* All business transactions form part of the BoP but the BoP also includes
non-business transactions such as aid transfers and family remittances.
Some exchanges actually occur *within* firms, that is the "buyer" and
"seller" are not independent of each other and might even be part of the
same legal entity. The BoP considers branches and subsidiaries (defined
below) of multinational enterprises to be separate entities.

1.1.1 What Makes a Business Transaction "International"?

Different criteria are used in different contexts (income taxation, tariffs)
but BoP determines nationality in a manner that allows us to apply it
non-arbitrarily to the full range of economic transactions. *A business
transaction is considered to be international if the entities involved reside in different countries.* Putting it in simple terms, when the payer's
address lists a different country from the recipient's address, the exchange is deemed international. Of course this just begs the question
of what we mean by the "address." For households, the residence is the
place where the members live on an indefinite basis.[3] For firms, it is
an establishment (factory, office) where it engages in the production of
goods and services.

Why should we use residency to determine whether an exchange
is international? An obvious alternative would be "nationality." This
might seem less ambiguous than residency, since we can just look and
see whether two parties have passports from different countries. Leaving
aside the fact that some individuals don't have passports and a few
have more than one, the standard of nationality would mean that all
purchases and earnings of migrants who have not changed citizenship

---

[3] For the BoP, the formal definition of residence is the "center of economic interest"
but the rule of thumb is that it takes a year in the foreign country for it to become
the new residence. There are many exceptions. For example, students abroad
and patients receiving treatment abroad are considered residents of their home
country as long as they are part of households there. As discussed in Chapter 12,
the rules that income taxation authorities use to determine residency are fairly
complicated.

would be viewed as international transactions. The nationality concept would be even more problematic for firms. On the one hand we could define nationality by country in which the firm is incorporated. Yet this would make a key distinction between subsidiaries (which would be considered nationals of the host country) and branches (nationals of the parent country). Alternatively, we could abandon legal definitions of a firms' nationalities and instead focus on the citizenship of the individuals who own and control the firm. This may not be practical for many multinational corporations since the individuals owning and controlling them come from many different countries. The concept of nationality remains important for taxation in some countries and also in some negotiations on "trade" in services. However, our default standard for defining transactions as international will be the BoP's residence rule.

For transactions involving goods, that is physical objects that can be moved from one country to another, there is a third criteria that is sometimes applied. It ignores the residences and nationalities of the parties involved in the transaction and instead examines whether the "origin" country differs from the "destination" country. Customs administrators determine the country goods come from through sometimes elaborate "rules of origin," discussed in Chapter 4. The origin test applied to goods works in practice the same as the residence test. This is because the producer of foreign-origin goods is deemed to be a foreign resident as long as it has a permanent establishment in that country.

1.1.2 Types of Transaction

The IMF *Balance of Payments Manual* breaks down transactions according to standard categories. We consider three types of transactions that are important for international business: trade, income, and investment.

Trade is the term commonly used to refer to international transactions involving products, that is, exports and imports of goods and services. There are three types of trade transactions.

- *Merchandise* transactions involve the transfer of ownership of a tangible and moveable object from a seller to a buyer.
- *Services* transactions are those in which a consumer benefits from actions taken by the service provider. Service transactions are extremely diverse and include transportation, communication, construction, accounting, advertising, research, entertainment, and some

insurance and financial services. Royalties and licence fees—the payments for authorized use of patents, trademarks, and copyrights—are also considered service transactions. Usual features of services are intangibility and the involvement of the consumer in the "production" of the service (think of haircuts, hotel room stays, and consulting).

- *Goods for processing* transactions send raw materials (e.g. crude oil, cotton thread) from country A to country B, where they undergo processing, and are then imported back into country A (e.g. as refined gas or t-shirts) *without* a transfer of ownership. Although this transaction appears to be an export of processing services from country B to A, the traditional book-keeping approach has been to consider the two distinct movements of goods (A to B, B to A) as *trade in goods*.

Income transactions are those involving the earnings and investment returns for a firms' employees, shareholders, and creditors. Employee compensation (wages, salaries, and benefits) transactions occur primarily between residents of the same country (the exception being workers on temporary assignments) so they are usually a very small component of net international income payments. The big categories of international income transactions are interest payments on debt and dividends for shareholders. Income and Trade receipts, net of payments, are the main determinants of most countries' *current accounts*.[4]

Investment transactions involve changes in ownership of assets. Figure 1.1 shows how to classify financial (stocks and bonds) investment transactions based on ownership shares.

- *Portfolio* investments in financial assets include equity securities (if owning less than 10% of the shares), debt securities and other financial instruments.
- *Direct* investment is the establishment or acquisition of an enterprise in which the investor intends to have a long-term relationship that includes an "effective voice in management," but not necessarily a "controlling interest." Since the actual objectives of investors may be difficult to discern, the IMF recommends that a 10% rule be applied to classify investments. If the investor owns 10% or more of an enterprise, then it should be deemed to be direct investment.

Direct investment is the transaction that defines a firm as a multinational enterprise so it is worth special attention. The first distinction

---

[4] The omitted component is transfers.

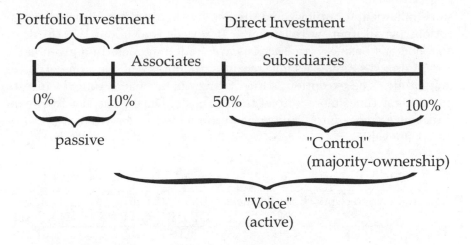

Fig. 1.1. IMF classifications for international investment

is between equity capital and reinvested earnings. Equity capital corresponds to investments in foreign affiliates known as *branches* when the unit is not separately incorporated, *associates* when the investing firm owns from 10% to 50% of the equity in a separately incorporated entity, and *subsidiaries* when the parent firm owns more than 50% (the usual requirement for "controlling interest") of the separately incorporated entity (also known as majority owned affiliates). Reinvested earnings are the enterprise earnings that are "deemed" to be paid out to the foreign investor but are reinvested rather than distributed. The IMF counts these earnings as additional direct investment, *as if* a dividend had been paid and a new investment made.

Although most investment transactions involve financial assets, another category that is conceptually important is the "acquisition of intangible assets." These correspond to transactions involving changes in ownership of patents, franchises, and other transferable contracts. The slightly confusing thing is that when a firm pays a foreign patent owner for the temporary rights to use the invention described in the patent (a license), this is considered trade in services. But if the same firm bought the patent itself (and thus obtained a permanent right to use the invention), this would be an investment transaction in intangible assets.

The magnitudes of the different international transactions are illustrated in Table 1.1 for the case of Canada in 2004.[5] The last column

---
[5] Data obtained online at http://www40.statcan.ca/l01/cst01/econ01a.htm.

sums inflows and outflows and divides by the total for all listed transactions (small items were left out). It reveals that about two thirds of all Canada's business transactions are trade in goods. In a given category, Canada's payments and receipts are mainly of the same order of magnitude. The exception is direct investment where Canada invests about eight times more abroad than it hosts. During the last five years direct investment into Canada has plummeted to less than a tenth of its 2000 level.

Table 1.1. Canada's international business transactions in 2004

Transaction	Receipts (Bn$) IN	Payments (Bn$) OUT	Balance IN−OUT	Shares (IN+OUT)/Total
Goods	429	363	66	67.5%
Services	62	74	−12	11.6%
Inv. Income	38	63	−25	8.6%
Portfolio Inv.	55	19	36	6.3%
Direct Inv.	8	62	−54	6.0%
Total	592	581	11	100.0%

1.1.3 Types of Entities

Having defined the different types of international business transactions, we should now consider the entities that carry out these activities. The three types of entities that concern us are defined below.

"Uninational" Enterprises: Firms that own permanent establishments and produce in only one country. These firms are also owned by domestic residents or as portfolio investment by foreign investors. Their sole forms of international business are importing and exporting in short-term transactions.

Multinational Contractual Networks: collections of sellers and buyers from different countries that are linked in long-term relationships but without significant cross-holdings of equity. Links take the form of contractual obligations. Examples include Nike and Reebok's relationships with the Asian firms to whom they sub-contract the manufacture of shoes, McDonald's network of franchised restaurants, and independent companies that bottle and distribute Coca Cola under license. Another type of contractual network involves agreements between firms that normally compete in the same industry. These combinations are often referred to as "alliances" and are common in the airline industry.

Multinational Enterprises: (MNEs) Any firm consisting of permanent establishments in more than one country, resulting from direct investment abroad by a "parent" firm that owns part or all of the constituent entities (called "direct investment enterprises" by the IMF) and has an effective voice in their management. One key activity of MNEs is the assignment of parent-company employees to work as "expatriates" in the FDI enterprises.

The largest MNES are legally organized as corporations and therefore referred to as Multinational Corporations (MNCs). For some reason, the United Nations calls these firms "transnational corporations" (TNCs) but that terminology has not been widely adopted. The largest MNCs are mainly producers of oil (Exxon-Mobil, Royal Dutch/Shell), autos (GM, Ford, Toyota), and electronics (General Electric, the current # 1). There are a few large MNEs that are not MNCs. A collection of offices that are jointly owned by a set of partners will be referred as Multinational Partnerships (MNPs). Prominent examples, all from the service sector, include auditing firms such as Ernst & Young, consulting firms such as McKinsey, and advertising firms such as Saatchi & Saatchi.

1.2 Six Forms of Separation

Globalization has been so persistently hyped (by its fans and critics) that many now talk as if we were all really living in a "global village." International business is indeed very important, especially in countries like Canada that export one third of what they produce and have extensive foreign ownership. Nevertheless we should still think of international business as being distinct from purely domestic business. There are a number of considerations that collectively differentiate international business. I call these the *six forms of separation*. The exact number and grouping of these distinctions is not very important (and indeed something that I have changed from earlier drafts). The key idea is that there are a number of related factors that make doing business across borders harder and riskier than doing it within national borders. Understanding these factors is essential for firms attempting to formulate a multinational strategy.

1.2.1 Political Separation

The political borders we see drawn on maps create the most obvious form of separation. Each nation has its own government that establishes and enforces its own laws.

One of the fundamental activities of national governments is to "secure" their political boundaries against "invasion" by unwanted people, products, financial transactions, and even ideas. Outward flows tend to cause less concern than inward flows; however, many governments do try to prevent so-called capital flight and all governments monitor outward flows of income to verify that relevant taxes have been paid.

The restrictions imposed on inward flows become apparent shortly after landing at a foreign airport. First, immigration officers try to restrict the movement of people. No nation that I am aware of has ever operated a fully open-door policy towards potential immigrants. Second, the would-be entrant must pass through customs, declaring which goods of foreign origin he wishes to enter the country with. Beyond certain limits, goods obtained abroad are subject to special taxes called tariffs or duties. Third, most international airports have foreign exchange counters where one can obtain the local currency. Most countries define a unique local form of money as the "sole legal tender" in that nation.

Temporary movement for the purposes of tourism is not very difficult and is actively encouraged by many countries. In some cases, such as the Canada-US FTA, countries have also facilitated movement of people who intend to supply services in the host country. Permanent movements are subject to more severe restrictions. Firms are usually legally required to give preference to domestic citizens in their hiring process when they are allowed to hire foreign workers at all.

Although tariffs have been lowered substantially over the last 35 years, especially by developed countries, exporters still face many important barriers. The difference is that barriers today are more likely to be triggered by actions of the exporter than before when they were part of a nation's overall trade policy. National governments also create a number of regulations that specify what goods and services can be sold and how they are to be produced. These regulations often have the effect of impeding provision of goods originating in countries with a different set of regulations. We will return to a discussion of protectionist trade policies in Chapters 4 and especially 5 and consider treatment of income flows by tax authorities in Chapter 12.

Inflows and outflows of financial capital used to be heavily restricted as well but now move fairly freely with a few important exceptions such as China. Canada is noteworthy in that it replaced its xenophobic Foreign Investment Review Agency with Investment Canada, an agency charged with attracting more investment. While internationally mobile capital draws much public attention today due to the rapidity and destabilizing consequences with which it moves from country to country, most capital remains in the country in which it is raised. The reasons for this are probably linked to forms of separation we will discuss subsequently.

Over the last half century there were three important trends in political separation. The first trend has increased the importance of political separation: there were 74 countries in 1950 and there are about 220 today. However, two other trends limit the power of these nations. Supra-national institutions were formed following World War II that exercised some influence on national policies. Despite extreme claims made by anti-globalization protestors, organizations like the United Nations, the World Trade Organization, International Monetary Fund still have only a limited amount of authority. The final trend is the proliferation of agreements between groups of countries to integrate their economies to varying extents. When they give up independent tariff policies, it is called a customs union. When they allow for free movement of labor and capital, it is referred to as a common market. Finally, a group of countries employing a common currency is called a monetary union.

1.2.2 Physical Separation

Countries are often separated from each other by physical barriers such as mountain ranges (the Himalayas, Andes, Pyrenees, Alps all coincide with at least one national border) and bodies of water (e.g. the English Channel, the Great Lakes). In addition, most nations are far away from most of the rest of the nations of the world. As a result, foreign producers and consumers are generally more distant than their domestic counterparts.

One of the most well-established empirical facts in international trade is that the further apart two countries are, the less they will trade. In fact, there is what might even be called an economic "law": trade is inversely proportionate to distance. A country that is 10% further away from you will import 10% less of your goods, holding all other things constant. Similar distance laws operate on the migration of people and the flows of foreign direct investment (FDI).

While the business-impeding effect of physical separation is well-established, the causes of distance's strong negative effect are not fully understood. Krugman has commented that "measured shipping costs are quite small for most goods that can be shipped at all; yet trade falls off quite sharply with distance. This suggests [a role for] transaction costs involving the difficulty of maintaining personal contact, or perhaps differences in culture that are correlated with physical distance."[6]

Historically, a major impediment for international business transactions was the physical cost of communicating information over long distances. Before telegraph and then telephone cables, people had to travel in order for information to travel over long distances.[7]

Krugman elaborates in the following quote about how communication technology can facilitate international trade.

> While it is not clear why distance plays so strong a role in trade, a common guess is that it proxies for the possibilities of personal contact between managers, customers, and so on; that much business depends on the ability to exchange more information, of a less formal kind, than can be sent over a wire. If this is true, then we might argue that the advent of such innovations as long-range passenger jets, cheap intercontinental telephone calls, fax machines, and electronic mail permit an intensity of long-distance business relationships that was not possible in 1913. Steamships may have been quite efficient at transporting bulk commodities, but they were too slow to allow regular visits to headquarters; telegraphs may have allowed effectively instantaneous communication of futures prices and interest rates, but they lacked the bandwidth to allow the home office to transmit detailed production specifications and the factory to explain why they would not work." (Krugman, 1995, "Growing World Trade" *Brookings Papers on Economic Activity*)

Communication costs also make it difficult to monitor and coordinate the activities of the overseas affiliates of multinational enterprises. Over time modern electronic methods of communication are making it much easier to transfer text, sounds, and images at low costs over great distances. However, business travel has continued to grow in importance. This suggests personal visits to conduct business overseas probably remain important. These visits still consume significant resources, the most important of which being the manager's valuable time.

---

[6] *Handbook of International Economics Volume 3*, page 1273. We consider the roles of personal contact and cultural differences in subsequent sections of this chapter.

[7] I am perhaps not giving enough credit to carrier pigeons and smoke signals.

We shall argue in Chapter 4 that conventional transportation costs are more significant than Krugman suggests. However, Krugman is probably right to argue that shipping costs are just one part of why physical geography matters. Another important reason—also discussed in Chapter 4—is shipping *time*. Time in transit is an important cost of doing business over long distances.

1.2.3 Relational Separation

Local communities have webs of one-on-one interactions that we call social and business networks. We care particularly about the case of business networks which comprise relationships between buyers and sellers. In the terminology of network analysis, buyers and sellers are called nodes. Some nodes are connected to each other with links. There are many types of links. For instance, in a telecommunication network, the links might be fiber optic cable. In a business network a link usually corresponds to an ongoing history of exchange. Relational separation occurs when buyers and sellers residing in one country are mainly linked to each other and have few if any links with their counterparts in a foreign country. Relational separation may not simply reflect an absence of past interactions. It is likely to also *cause* a reluctance to engage in future interactions. This is because buyers and sellers that are already connected tend to prefer to continue to trade with each other and they often shun "outsiders," those they have never interacted with before. One of the main activities of business networks is the spread of information. Members of the network transmit specific bits of useful information to each other. Examples of such "data sharing" include

leads: names of people who can provide (or who need) particular items. Most goods are not sold on organized markets and buyers must search for a product that meets their requirements. As a result of their own past searches and informal communication, other members of the network can refer the searcher to a seller they have discovered that makes the desired product.

blacklists: names of people who are known to be untrustworthy. The fact that businessmen can use their local connections to find out who has breached contracts in the past allows them to be more secure in signing contracts. Their lack of connections in foreign countries means that they do not know reputations and this increase *transaction costs* (see Chapter 4).

1.2.4 Environmental Separation

Individuals in different countries often behave quite differently. They produce and demand different products. One fundamental source of such differences is that countries differ in their natural environments. Here we have in mind differences in temperature, rainfall, altitude, water availability, soil types, and mineral resources. Large countries like Canada and Brazil also exhibit huge environmental variation within their borders. Nevertheless, nowhere in Canada can one economically grow bananas or coffee. Correspondingly, there is nowhere in Brazil where consumers demand snow tires for their cars.

As a general rule, nearby countries have more similar environments. Think of the oil-rich—and water-poor—nations of the Middle East. However, environmental differences are not a simple function of distance. One key determinant of temperature is latitude. Countries further from the equator have colder winters, cooler summers and also larger ranges in temperature. Tropical countries also seem to suffer from a more debilitating set of diseases, with malaria being the most prominent example. Due to these latitude effects, regions as far apart as Bordeaux, France and Hunter Valley, Australia grow wines with similar grapes.

The examples above suggest two conflicting effects of environmental separation on international business, and in particular trade in goods. Countries with different environments will often have greater opportunities to trade with each other because they will have one set of goods in abundance while another, scarce in their own country, will be abundant elsewhere. We consider this idea in greater depth in Chapter 3. In contrast, environment-induced differences in demands will tend to limit trade opportunities (Chapter 6). Scottish wool sweaters will not be sought after in Indonesia (unless air conditioning becomes much much more prevalent)!

1.2.5 Developmental Separation

Countries differ dramatically in their levels of economic development. For instance, in Indonesia, notorious host to many of the "sweatshops" that sew together shoes for Nike, about 8% of its 209 million population (i.e. over 16 million) live on less than one U.S. dollar per day. These figures seem small, however, when contrasted with much of Africa. Africa's largest country, Nigeria, home to 111 million, has 70% of its population

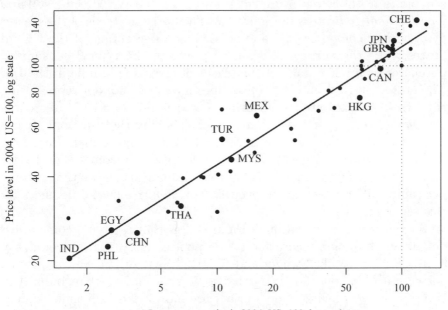

Fig. 1.2. Richer countries are also more expensive

living on less than a dollar per day.[8] Life expectancy at birth is under 52 years in Nigeria, in contrast to 66 years in Indonesia, and about 79 years in Canada, Australia, and most of Scandinavia.

All the statistics in the preceding paragraph reflect 1999 data reported in the United Nation's *Human Development Indicators* which can be downloaded from the UN website. This document also reports on other indicators of human development such as literacy, access to clean water, and female participation in the economic and political spheres. The UN averages across several categories to generates a single number it calls the Human Development Index. One of the chief components of the index—and the one that economists tend to focus on—is income per capita. This focus is not as narrow-minded as it might sound because income per capita is highly correlated with many of the other indicators of development. Rich countries have higher education levels, better health, more extensive infrastructure, etc.

Higher levels of income per capita are also strongly associated with higher consumer price levels. This fact is illustrated for the fifty largest

---

[8] There are, at this time, no Nike factories in Nigeria(http://www.nike.com/nikebiz/nikebiz.jhtml?page=25&cat=activefactories).

economies in the world using 2004 data from the World Bank's *World Development Indicators* in Figure 1.2. The horizontal axis of the scatter plot shows income per capita expressed as a percentage of the United States while the vertical axis shows prices of the typical consumers' purchases as a percentage of the prices of the same bundle in the US. The dotted vertical and horizontal lines intersect on a dot representing the US. Both axes are shown using a "log scale" in which differences correspond to proportional changes. That is why the gap from 10 and 20 is the same as the gap from 50 to 100. The figure includes a best fit line. Its slope tells us that each 10% rise in income leads to 4% higher prices. Furthermore, the statistical analysis shows that income per capita differences explain over 90% of the price level differences for this set of countries.

An important implication of Figure 1.2 is that a given income in US dollars will buy many more goods in a poor country, than it would, say in a rich country like Switzerland (CHE).[9] Switzerland has an income per capita (48 thousand USD) that is 75 times larger than India (640 USD). However, Switzerland's prices are more than 7.35 times higher. This means that the purchasing power of the average Swiss income is about *ten* times larger than the average Indian—a large multiple, certainly, but not nearly as large as the unadjusted income ratio.

The observation that prices rise with incomes is called the "Penn Effect" because the group of economists that documented this result was based at the University of Pennsylvania. Because of the Penn Effect we should not compare the income per capita of one country to another without taking into account price differences. Incomes expressed in "purchasing power parity (PPP) dollars" are adjusted for price differences and are sometimes called "real" incomes. We will return to the concept of PPP and examine how market exchange rates relate to PPP exchange rates in Chapter 10.

Figure 1.3 depicts the incomes of the 52 largest economies of the world as a staircase. The height of each step corresponds to income per capita in PPP US$. The width of each step is proportional to the population of each country. Thus, the area under each step corresponds to total income or gross national income (GNI) of each country. We see dramatic differences in real incomes across countries. The long horizontal line shows the hypothetical income that would result from

---

[9] ISO codes are standard abbreviations, available online at http://en.wikipedia.org/wiki/ISO_3166-1_alpha-3. While most of them are fairly easy to figure out, CHE is puzzling until you learn that Switzerland's Latin name is *Confoederatio Helvetica*.

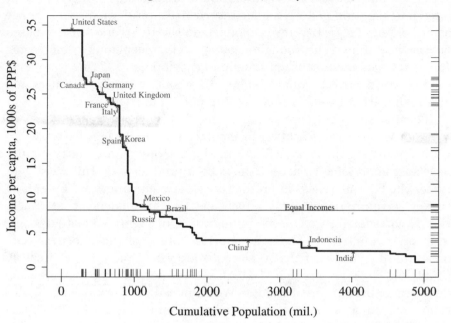

Fig. 1.3. The distribution of world income

redistributing all the world's income equally (assuming, in a wildly un-realistic way, that such a thing could be accomplished costlessly). We would all have to settle (in this imaginary world) with the standard of living currently enjoyed by the average Russian or Brazilian.

These figures point to one of the most important issues in the world today: Why are citizens of some countries so much richer (on average) than citizens of other countries? Many people think they know the answer but no single answer is fully satisfactory. To begin thinking about the issues, it is useful to break down income per capita into its underlying determinants. First total income is just the sum of wage earnings and investment income. If there are L active workers paid an average of w in annual wages and a capital stock of K generate annual investment returns of r_K, then the total income a country is given by

$$Y = wL + r_K K.$$

Dividing by the population, N, we obtain income per capita of

$$y = Y/N = w(L/N) + r_K(K/N).$$

This gives a simple answer to the question of why some countries are rich: they must have some combination of higher wages, higher labour force participation (L/N), higher returns to capital, or higher average asset holdings (K/N). Many economists in the 1950s and 1960s focused on the last item. The thought that "capital deepening" (increasing K/N) was the main cause of economic development. If this were true, solving world poverty would mainly be about increasing savings and also reallocating loanable funds to the poor countries.

There is now widespread consensus that capital deepening is not enough. Most of the variation in incomes per capita can be traced to variation in wages. As we will see in the Chapter 2, a country cannot have sustainably high wages without high productivity. But what generates the big differences in productivity between countries? One thing that is certainly important is education. But for evidence that education is not enough, we can see immigration of highly educated people from poor countries to the rich countries. Many of these migrants are motivated by the belief that their skills are worth more in the wealthy countries. The reason is that the high income per capita countries have, on average, better "institutions." We cannot delve very deep into this topic here but is an area of active research among economists. One of the strong findings is that there is a remarkably tight relationship between various measures of the rules of society and income per capita. Richer countries tend to have stronger legal institutions than poorer countries. They are more likely to have democratically elected governments (the exceptions being mainly oil-rich nations) and to have lower rates of crime and corruption.

Corruption is something that is very hard to define, but most of us feel we know it when we see it. The Wikipedia defines corruption as "the misuse of public power for illegitimate, usually secret, private advantage." World Bank economists Kaufmann, Kraay, and Mastruzzi aggregated data from 31 different organizations to rate every country on perceptions of how well it manages to control corruption. Figure 1.4 plots corruption differences with respect to the US against relative incomes (not corrected for price differences). We observe a very strong relationship: higher incomes per capita are associated with lower perceived corruption. A reasonable inference is that if somehow a country can find a way to control corruption, then its economy can perform at a higher level, generating more wealth. Unfortunately, the ability to control corruption may be a consequence of historical and cultural events that took place decades or even centuries ago.

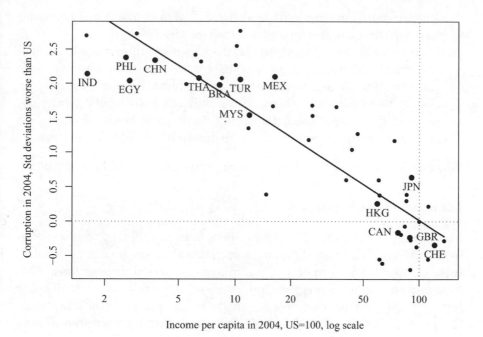

Fig. 1.4. Higher income countries have better control of corruption

After this rather superficial investigation of why incomes differ so greatly, we should now ask how income differences matter for the strategies of multinational enterprises. I see five important mechanisms.

1. Poor countries are much more likely to disintegrate into civil wars or even anarchy (Rwanda, Somalia, and Afghanistan are recent cases).
2. The ubiquity of corruption also raises the costs of doing business for the MNE's subsidiaries. Although some firms may be tempted to use the corruptibility of public officials to their advantage, local firms will usually hold the advantage.
3. Managers from rich countries will generally view work in poor countries as a hardship due to these countries' relatively undeveloped physical and legal infrastructures. The MNE must generally offer its employees extra compensation to induce them to accept assignments in poor countries.
4. The typical consumer in a rich country has very different demands from those in poor countries. Many goods exhibit strong positive income effects. Demand for some goods, called "luxuries," increases more than proportionately with income. Examples include cars, di-

amond rings, and perhaps health care. Meanwhile, poor countries have relatively high demand for "necessities."

5. Differences in average incomes reflect in part differences in human and physical capital per person. Rich and poor countries will have gains from trade associated with their differences in "factor proportions." In particular rich countries will tend to export goods and services that allow them to exploit their high levels of education and capital, while importing goods made by unskilled labourers.

We consider many of the issues above in greater detail in later chapters.

1.2.6 Cultural Separation

Not all differences in the behavior of people from different countries can be attributed solely to differences in natural environment or wealth. Instead, there is an important role played by social interactions. This final form of separation is easy and interesting to talk about informally but very difficult to analyze rigorously. Furthermore, even more than the prior forms of separation, cultural separation embraces an almost overwhelming diversity of phenomena.

We are all aware of the stereotypical ways that citizens of different nations are reported to differ. They are even the subject of many jokes. One that I believe unlikely to be considered offensive goes as follows: "Q. What's the difference between Heaven and Hell? A. Heaven is where the police are English, the bankers are Swiss, and the cooks are Italian. Hell is where the cooks are English, the police are Swiss, and the bankers are Italian." The notion behind the joke is that certain characteristics of these different European groups lead them to be good at some occupations and bad at others. These attributes do not seem like responses to environmental differences. Rather, to the extent they are real, they are presumably cultural inheritances.

Many claims about national cultures amount to little more than crude stereotyping. We should always recognize that huge variation exists *within* countries. Furthermore, we should be skeptical of simplistic explanations of cultural differences. For example, in Deresky's (2003) *International Management: Managing Across Borders and Cultures*, we obtain (on page 109) the following account of German culture:

> Christianity underlies much of German culture—more than 96 percent of Germans are Catholics or Protestants. This may be why Germans tend to like rule and order in their lives, and why there is a clear public expectation of the acceptable and the

unacceptable way to do things. Public signs everywhere in Germany dictate what is allowed or "verboten" (forbidden). Germans are very strict with their use of time, whether for business or pleasure, frowning on inefficiency or tardiness."

This quote raises a couple of issues. First, can we believe the reported religiosity of the Germans? The CIA World Factbook lists just 68% of Germans as Christians. Presumably this is based on self-descriptions. It may not characterize actual beliefs and practices. The Pew Research Center conducted a survey in 2002 that found that only 21% of Germans said that "religion plays a very important role in their lives." Suppose we overlooked these problems and were willing to stipulate that Germans are very Christian. We still should not infer that this would explain their supposed insistence on order and punctuality. The CIA Factbook shows that 89% percent of Brazilians are Christians and the Pew Center found that 77% considered religion very important. Although the data show them to be more Christian than Germans, few visitors to Brazil would form the opinion that Brazilians relish order and punctuality. If there really are fundamental differences between Germans and Brazilians on these issues, they almost certainly *do not* arise from differences in the prevalence of the Christian religion.

How then can we explain German punctuality? It seems likely that most Germans today are both punctual and Christian because they inherited these attributes from their parents who inherited from theirs, and so on. In addition, Germans *have* to be punctual because they interact on a regular basis with other Germans who are punctual and expect it of others. A German who moved to Brazil might well gradually find himself slipping on his timeliness after he arrived at a few social invitations on time only to find the hosts still taking their showers.

These two explanations for German punctuality correspond to the two principle mechanisms of "cultural transmission" discussed by Luigi Luca Cavalli-Sforza (1999). This geneticist suggested an analogy with biological mechanisms of transmission. One is the "vertical" method, by which one generation passes on characteristics to the following one. In biology, the primary vertical mechanism is the inheritance of genes. In society, the vertical mechanism is something we might call "traditions." Examples include recipes, home remedies for illness, and religions. The second mechanism is horizontal transfer between members of the same generation. The biological example is the spread of a virus from host to host through infection. We will discuss both mechanisms in turn.

While biologists now have a very clear understanding of how genes are passed on, we have little precision in understanding vertical cultural transmission. The basic idea is that parents instruct their children at an age in which they are "impressionable." The mechanism seems to be one of "imprinting." During childhood, tastes, like the ability to learn a language, are flexible and respond to stimuli from parents. Over time children become accustomed to certain levels of sweetness in chocolate, or tenderness in meat. Once established, these preferences may be difficult to shake in adulthood and then be passed on to the next generation. If citizens in one country prefer their products to have certain attributes that are not considered desirable in other nations, this may create an impediment for foreign suppliers. Cavalli-Sforza presents some evidence to support the idea that children tend to acquire the religion of their mother and the political party affiliation of their father.

The role of parental instruction explains why some families might be consistently Christian or even consistently punctual across generations but why are German families in general different from Brazilian families? *Differences between nations arise when most or all of the people in a nation share a common set of relatively recent ancestors who were not the ancestors of most people in the other nation.* We can see this "common heritage" effect most clearly by considering one example of culture that has been transmitted vertically in most countries: the surnames of men. Names like Zhang and Li are much more common in China than in Spain where names like Garcia and Martinez are more common. Another example, more relevant for international business is that initial instruction in language is done by parents. Thus, the words we use in different countries tend to be similar to the words used by our common ancestors.

Differences in culture have important effects on the employment relationships at overseas affiliates of multinational enterprises. In general, it may be difficult to simply replicate practices that work well in one country to another country. As a very trivial example, a nine to five work day might be the norm in countries colonized by England but, in countries colonized by Spain, there is often the expectation of an afternoon nap (or *siesta*) period prior to restarting work.

The vertical mechanism of cultural transmission is important but it tends to acquire real force when combined with horizontal mechanisms. The latter operate between peers, or members of the same generation. Individuals tend to share beliefs and behaviour patterns with other members of the groups with whom they interact. There are a number of reasons for such conformity. The first might be a simple instinct to imitate. "Monkey see, monkey do" is a saying that conveys the idea of mindless imitation. In reality, humans *and* monkeys are more sophis-

ticated. Some Japanese researchers have studied the social behaviour
of macaque monkeys. One of their remarkable findings was a young
female named Imo who introduced a method for cleaning the grain
given to them by researchers. She dropped it in water at which point
the dirt would sink. Soon other juvenile monkeys picked up this trick
and then it spread to the adults. This example illustrates the idea that
much imitation arises through learning from the examples of others.
This monkey example suggests a possibly useful dichotomy for thinking about imitation.

Conformism: The imitator's final objective is simply to conform with
    behaviour of others. That is the key desire is just to "fit in" with
    what others are doing.
Social learning: I copy you, not because I want to be like you, but
    because we are both trying to solve the same problem and I believe
    your solution will work for me too. For instance, I might be trying to
    choose a restaurant in an unfamiliar neighborhood. I might follow
    others into a crowded restaurant even if I don't like crowds because
    I think that they know the restaurant is good.

A third type of imitation arises from the benefits of coordinating on
"conventions." In order to be compatible, members of a group adhere
to standards. Examples of conventions include

- rules of the road: driving on the right hand side in France but on
  the left hand side in Britain in order to avoid head-on collisions.
- manners: the incentive to be punctual depends strongly on whether
  the other people convening at a pre-announced time are expected
  to be punctual. A Brazilian who moves to Germany will find it in
  his interest to be more on time in Frankfurt than he would be in
  Rio de Janeiro.
- languages: sounds and written characters that facilitate communication. The word "dog" is a convention used to refer to a particular species of furry, four-legged carnivores. The words "cachorro,"
  "perro," and "chien" would serve equally well. Indeed it is a convention to read from left to right. Without this convention we wouldn't
  be able to distinguish between the animal and the deity.
- currencies: tokens that can be used to obtain valuable goods instead of relying upon barter. Their usefulness depends crucially on
  whether other people view them as valuable.
- systems of measurement: kilos, liters, inches, etc. The value of conventions can be illustrated by a case where there is none: bales of

hay. When you pay $6 for a bale you may obtain 100 pounds worth or just 30!

- product interfaces: plugs for electricity connections, paper types (A4 vs 8.5-by-11 inches), etc.

We will return to the issue of conventions and their importance in Chapter 6. Currencies are the topic of Chapter 10. For now, note that horizontal pressures to conform tend to help lock in place patterns of behavior and belief that were first learned from parents. I was born in Germany to American parents. The first language I learned was my parents' language. However, had we stayed in Germany, I would probably have come to prefer and be more competent in German, the language of my peers. Parental transmission and peer influence work together strongly when people do not migrate very far from their birthplace.

1.3 Looking Forward

The six forms of separation can matter for domestic business, especially in large, varied countries. But they will usually be *vital* issues for international business. Thus the study of multinational strategy is the study of making business decisions when the six forms of separation are important.

The book proceeds as follows. Like most firms, we begin with exporting and importing, and tackle issues raised by overseas investment later. We first analyze the gains from trade and then enumerate the many costs of cross-border goods and service transactions. Next we apply the four elements of multinational strategy—*factor advantages*, *trade costs*, *scale economies*, and *market sizes*—to the decision of which multinational form best suits each firm. We then take up issues of central importance to firms that invest overseas: exchange rate risk, political risk, taxation, and expatriate assignments.

References

Cavalli-Sforza, Luigi Luca, 1999, *Genes, Peoples, Languages*.
Central Intelligence Agency, 2006, *World Fact Book* http://www.cia.gov/cia/publications/factbook/
Deresky, Helen, 2003, *International Management: Managing Across Borders and Cultures*, 4th ed., Prentice Hall: New Jersey.

Kaufmann, Daniel, Aart Kraay, and Massimo Mastruzzi, 2005, "Governance Matters IV: Governance Indicators for 1996–2004." The World Bank.

Pew Research Center, 2002, "Among Wealthy Nations U.S. Stands Alone In Its Embrace Of Religion" http://people-press.org/reports/

Gains from Trade

The days when raw materials were produced in one country and turned into finished goods in another are long gone. The making of even the simplest goods is chopped up into a number of different stages, reflecting relative costs in different countries and falling international transport costs. Charlie Woo, chief executive of Megatoys, explains how a childs pinwheel, consisting of plastic sails pinned to a stick, is made in three different countries. The plastic is produced in America and cut to shape in China. The toy is then assembled in Mexico and shipped to LA for distribution.[1]

Imagine yourself as a recently promoted manager for Bel Canto, a Milan headquartered women's shoe company. Bel Canto sources its shoes from two factories it operates in Asia. Each factory has 300 workers under contract for the whole year. The workers in each factory have the capability to spend their time making *either* soles *or* sewing together uppers (including, adding the soles, to complete the shoe). The following productivity table provides the essential information for analyzing short-run decisions.

Keep in mind that each worker can accomplish only one task or another on a given day. Thus the same Korean worker *cannot* make both 200 uppers and 200 soles. She must make 200 uppers *or* 200 soles.

---

[1] "An angelic mix," October 1st 1998, *The Economist*

Table 2.1. Productivity table: Output per worker per day

		Activity: Uppers	Soles
Factory:	Korea	200	400
	Thailand	100	100

2.1 Comparative Advantage in the Short Run

Decide what task (making soles or uppers) to assign to each worker in the Korea and Thailand plants. The 300 workers are under contract in each country and cannot be laid off in the short run. As a consequence, costs are fixed outside of your control. To maximize profits therefore you must focus on maximizing revenues. Assume that soles and uppers are light weight and compact so transportation costs can be reasonably ignored. Furthermore, you are a small player in the shoe industry and face a given market price for the shoes you make. Taken together these assumptions imply that you can focus on maximizing output and the result will maximize profits as well. You now prepare a plan for what activity each worker in each plant should execute.

Consider 4 plans:

Plan A: The previous manager had instructed each plant to manufacture complete shoes only. That is, he had made each plant self-sufficient (or "stand-alone" or *autarkic*): makers of uppers received all their soles from the same plant. In Thailand, the equal productivities mean that the labour force can be split in two: 150 workers on soles and the rest making uppers. Thailand will make 15,000 shoes per day. In Korea 2 workers will be making uppers for every one in soles. Thus there will be 100 workers doing soles, 200 making uppers, and total output will be 40,000. *The company's total output will be 55,000 shoes.*

Plan B: Let Thailand specialize in uppers and import soles from Korea who will specialize in soles. By focusing on uppers, Thailand can make 30,000 of them. Koreans will therefore need to supply 30,000 soles. However this will require only 75 workers, leaving 225 idle, or they will make soles that have no upper and are therefore useless.

Recall that your contractual obligations prevent you from laying these workers off. *Total company output is 30,000 shoes.*

Plan B*: Let Thailand specialize in uppers, yielding 30,000 uppers as in Plan B. The Korean plant will use 150 workers to make 60,000 soles. The other 150 workers will make 30,000 more uppers. Combining them all together we obtain a *total output of 60,000 shoes.*

Plan C (reverse of B*): Let Thailand specialize in soles—it will be able to make 30,000 of them. The Korean plant would assign 250 workers to uppers, making 50,000 of them. The remaining 50 workers would make 20,000 soles. *Total output would be 50,000 shoes.*

Comparing across the plans, we see that Plan B* yields the most shoes. By implementing this plan, we increase total shoe production by 5000 shoes relative to the previous plan of self-sufficient factories. Note that this implies a gain in productivity from roughly 91 shoes per worker per day to 100 shoes per day. From a certain perspective this 10% productivity gain is remarkable. There is no new machinery at use; no innovations to the production process have been introduced; no inspirational scheme has motivated workers to try harder. The gains draw entirely from the introduction of *trade*. Instead of being self-reliant, the Thai plant now imports soles from the Korean plant. While specialization is incomplete (the Korean plant makes some uppers), the plants are more integrated than under Plan A.

Another remarkable fact is that we found gains from trade even though the Korean plant has an absolute advantage in both activities.

Absolute Advantage: An individual (or plant or country) has absolute advantage in producing X if he or she can produce a unit of that good with fewer resources expended than other individuals. Equivalently, we could say absolute advantage comes from being able to produce more output from the same amount of inputs.

The example shows that specialization and trade can give rise to gains even if one plant is "better" at both tasks than the other plant. However, specialization and trade do not automatically generate benefits; the pattern of specialization is not arbitrary here. In fact there are losses from the wrong specialization plan (Plan C). In this example the losses from mis-specialization (5,000 shoes) are as large as the gains from correct specialization.

How does the firm choose which specialization plan to follow? One way to proceed is trial and error. However, there is an easier way to decide between Plans A, B*, and C. Let the least productive plant (in terms of absolute advantages) specialize in its comparative advantage activity. Then the more efficient plant can partially specialize in its comparative advantage.

Comparative Advantage: An individual (or plant or country) has comparative advantage in the production of X if the opportunity cost of producing more X is lower for that individual than for others.

The opportunity costs of making soles—that is, the number of uppers that must be foregone to produce an extra sole—in Korea and Thailand are:

Thailand: take 1 worker out of uppers you lose 100 uppers but gain 100 soles. Thus the opportunity cost of sole production is $100/100 = 1$ upper per sole.

Korea: take 1 worker out of upper production and you lose 200 uppers and gain 400 soles. Thus the opportunity cost of sole production is $200/400 = 1/2$ upper per sole. Korea has lower opportunity cost of sole production and hence a comparative advantage in that activity.

2.2 Comparative Advantage in the Long Run

What about the Long Run? Contracts with the workers will be completed and then the firm must decide again how many workers to hire in each plant. To keep things simple, we assume that both factories are completely paid off and the factory equipment has no salvage value, i.e. disregard capital costs and concentrate on labour costs.

1. How low would the wage have to be in Thailand for you to want to shut down the Korean plant?
2. How high would the wage have to be in Thailand for you to opt to use only the Korean plant?
3. What do you do if the wage is between those levels?
4. Suppose the wages are fixed by government legislation at 100 Baht per worker in Thailand and 200 Won per worker in Korea. What range of exchange rates (defined in Baht/Won) would you predict for Korea and Thailand?
5. Suppose productivity of the Thai workers doubles in both activities. Suppose you negotiate with a labour representative on the wage. What do you predict the new wage will be?

To answer these questions we need to calculate unit labour costs (ULC). *The unit labour cost is the wage divided by productivity.*

We denote the Thai wage as W_T and the Korean wage expressed in Won as W_K. To make monetary costs comparable, they must be measured in a common currency. It does not matter which one and we will work in the Thai currency, the Baht. The Korean wage expressed in Baht is eW_K, where e measures *Baht per Won*.

Table 2.2. Unit labour costs: Baht per sole or Baht per upper

| | | Activity: | |
		Uppers	Soles
Factory:	Korea	$eW_K/200$	$eW_K/400$
	Thailand	$W_T/100$	$W_T/100$

For Thailand to have cheaper unit labour costs in both tasks, the following conditions must be met:

Thai Plant Cheaper for Uppers: $W_T/100 < eW_K/200$ or $eW_K/W_T > 2$.
Thai Plant Cheaper for Soles: $W_T/100 < eW_K/400$ or $eW_K/W_T > 4$.

Thus if the Korean wage (expressed in Baht) is 4 times larger than the Thai wage, Korea's higher productivity will not be sufficient to offset its higher wages. Consequently, it would make sense to shut down the Korean plant and manufacture complete shoes in Thailand. On the other hand, if Korean wages were less than double Thai wages, then the Korean plant would have lower costs in both activities and it would make sense to shut down the Thai plant.

Figure 2.1 illustrates the relative costs and the corresponding optimal strategy for different values of the Korean wage expressed relative to the Thai wage (in a common currency, of course). For the intermediate range of $2 < eW_K/W_T < 4$, the Thai plant is low cost for uppers and the Korean plant is low cost for soles. Hence, both plants should be kept open, each one fully specialized in the activity of its comparative advantage. Note that the Thai plant will have four times as many workers so that they can make enough uppers for each sole produced by the Korean workers. Suppose for instance that you maintained the 300 workers in Korea while boosting Thai employment to 1200. Then it would be possible to produce 120,000 shoes. In contrast, if the two fac-

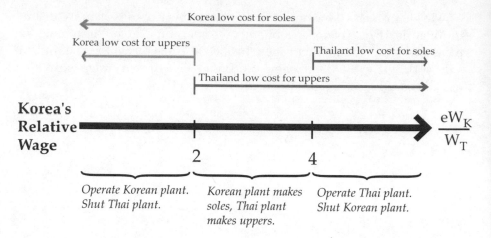

Fig. 2.1. Relative wage bands

tories were run on a "stand-alone" basis, total output would be 100,000 shoes (40,000 from Korea and 60,000 from Thailand). Thus, if the work force in Thailand were large enough to allow for *complete specialization*, the gain in output from exploiting comparative advantage would be 20%, considerably more than the 10% short-run gain.

Suppose we are provided with wages in each home country that are fixed in home currency units (perhaps the legal minimum wage or the workers' opportunity costs in the non-traded sector). For example suppose $W_T = 100$ Baht and $W_K = 200$ Won. Substituting into our condition for keeping both plants open we obtain $2 < 2e < 4$. Dividing by 2, this reduces to $1 < e < 2$ Baht/Won. If the exchange rate were to rise to over 2 (a depreciation of the Baht relative to the Won), the Korean shoe factories would be priced out of the market. Korean exports would decline and pressure would come to bear against the Won. If the shoe industry or other industries with similar relative productivities were an important source of Korea's export earnings, the downward pressure on the Won would eventually force it back down. A similar sequence would occur if e fell below 1. Then Thailand would be unable to compete in either good so there would be downward pressure on Baht (upward pressure on Won).

What would be the effect of a productivity increase? To maintain both countries active in the shoe industry, the relative wage cannot exceed the relative productivity for both soles and uppers. With the doubling of productivity in Thailand, we replace the condition $2 < eW_K/W_T < 4$ with $1 < eW_K/W_T < 2$. Put another way, the Thai wage cannot be greater than the Korean wage (or it would not be competitive in uppers), but it should not be less than half of the Korean wage (or it would take both activities).

2.3 The Shoe Story and Economic Reality

What do we learn from this problem?

1. Differences in wages (and living standards) across countries will tend to reflect differences in their average productivities (i.e. absolute advantages). The realism of this point is supported by Stephen Golub's research which is described in the *Economist* article "Not so absolutely fabulous" (November 4th, 1995). The data (from 1990) show that the much lower wages paid to workers in the Philippines, India, Thailand and Malaysia are offset by low productivity. US wages are somewhat more than five times the amounts paid in those countries, but productivity is five times higher as well. Korean wages are higher, about one third the US level, compared with productivity in manufacturing that averages 40% of the US. As a result, unit labour costs are no lower in these low-wage countries than they are in the US.

2. Even a country with an absolute disadvantage in the production of every good will not have a *comparative* disadvantage in every good. It will tend to export the goods where it has comparative advantage. The key point is that industries differ in their relative productivities but pay roughly the same wages for similar workers. Thus, all industries in Malaysia pay wages that are about 15% of US levels. On average, productivity is 15% of US levels. However, in some industries, the productivity gap is much narrower. As a result, Malaysia has a unit labour cost advantage in those industries and will tend to export them. Examples include VCRs, radios, telephone sets.

3. High-wage and low-productivity countries gain from trading with each other.

4. Exchange rates ultimately adjust to levels that are consistent with the pattern of comparative advantage.

What is missing from the account presented in this chapter? We have no understanding yet of the sources of comparative advantage. The implicit idea is that the primary difference between countries are the industry-specific skills of that country's workers. Yet, where do those skills come from? Furthermore, goods in the real world are made from factors in addition to labour. How does consideration of land, capital, climate, and mineral resources affect comparative advantage? Finally, how does comparative advantage change over time? One theory is that the first country to gain comparative advantage gets a permanent *first-mover* advantage. Another theory is that comparative advantage follows a predictable "life-cycle." We will explore these issues in the following chapter.

2.4 From Comparative to Competitive Advantage

What is a "competitive advantage" and how does it differ from the "comparative advantages" we have been discussing? Essentially a "competitive advantage" is the ability to beat your competitors at something. In war, competitive advantage often comes from better weapons. In the marketplace, competitive advantage usually arises from offering a product with a more attractive set of attributes. To be concrete, let us say that firm 1 has a competitive advantage over firm 2 with respect to consumer X if firm 1 can offer X a product that delivers greater consumer surplus than the product offered by firm 2. The maximum consumer surplus available is where firm i supplies the product at its marginal cost, c_i. Mathematically, that means $v_1 - c_1 > v_2 - c_2$, where the v are the amounts that Ms. X "values" the product. This says that firm 1's competitive advantage could come from a better (more appealing) product, i.e. $v_1 > v_2$ or from lower costs $c_1 < c_2$ *or some combination.*[2] In this chapter we have focused on how comparative advantage can give rise to a cost advantage. In the shoe story we say that a country has a competitive advantage when its *unit labour cost* is lower. The same ideas could be reformulated to show a location could achieve comparative advantage in terms of quality.

The important distinction between comparative advantage and competitive advantage is that comparative advantage exists no matter what wages and exchange rates happen to be. This is because comparative advantage is the outcome of differences in relative productivities. These productivities are usually expressed in terms of more units of output per unit of input. However, one could take into account quality of the output produced in calculations of productivity and it would remain

---

[2] One annoying thing in many strategy discussions is the presumption that you have to choose to have a better product or else to have lower costs. This is the Ferrari-Yugo choice. Many firms succeed by making a good product that they can sell at an affordable price. Think of Toyota, for example. It doesn't offer the highest v but it also isn't the lowest c: it succeeds by being good on both fronts.

a concept of comparative advantage. Competitive advantage, on the other hand, *does* take into account the actual set of prevailing wages (and other factor prices) and exchange rates. Thus a location could obtain a competitive advantage from relatively high productivity or from relatively low wages. Now a firm choosing the right location to produce something cares *directly* about competitive advantage. In the long run wages and exchange rates adjust so as to give a production location a competitive advantage in the same activities as it has a comparative advantage. It makes sense to think about comparative advantage because there can be temporary disturbances that push wages or exchange rates away from the levels they should be. This can temporarily give competitive advantages to industries that lack comparative advantage. A firm planning on making a long term investment or long term contractual relationship with a supplier should avoid being lured by such transitory competitive advantages (or disadvantages).

There is another distinction between comparative and competitive advantages. When we speak of comparative advantages, we usually refer to workers in specific locations (the Korean and Thai factories in our example). Firms do not have comparative advantages in the same way that workers do. Why not? Well, unlike a worker with a fixed number of working hours available for different tasks or a country with a given work force, the firm is able to grow or shrink by hiring or firing workers. Thus, the firm can expand production in all activities simultaneously by adding more workers. This makes the concept of opportunity cost difficult to apply to firms. Only a firm with some resource that it cannot adjust will have comparative advantage because then when it devotes more of that resource to one activity, it has to cut back on the other.[3] Remember, opportunity cost is the key determinant of comparative advantage. Firms *do* have competitive advantages that depend on the wages and productivities (taking into account product quality) of the workers employed by the firm. And that brings us to another way to express one of the key points of this chapter: *a firm that exploits comparative advantage (via factory specialization) can obtain a competitive advantage over firms that do not.*

2.5 Shoe Story II: Returns to Scale

Comparative advantage is one of the two main generators of gains from trade. Essentially, it says "Concentrate production in the *right* place."

---

[3] In Chapter 8 we consider the idea that the attention of the top management team is a fixed resource that can give rise to firm-level comparative advantage.

The other generator is something called returns to scale. Also phrased as a command, it says "Concentrate production in *one* place."

We can illustrate the gains to trade that come from exploiting returns to scale by modifying the shoe story. In contrast to assuming differences between the Thai and Korean workers, now we assume they are exactly alike in terms of their productivity and wages. No matter the task, each worker involved in production creates 100 uppers or soles per day. In this case opportunity costs are identical (1 upper per sole) and there is no gain from trade based on comparative advantage. The firm must divide its 600 workers 50-50, with 300 on each task, yielding $300 \times 100 = 30000$ shoes per day. Whether factories specialize or are self-sufficient makes no difference in this case.

Table 2.3. Productivity table II: Output per *production worker* per day

| | | Activity: | |
		Uppers	Soles
Factory:	Korea	100	100
	Thailand	100	100

The situation changes completely if we introduce the idea of *indivisible* "overhead." To produce any uppers at all in a given factory, a minimum of 30 workers must be set aside from production. These overhead workers may be thought as being engaged in accounting, material purchases, machinery maintenance, or some similar task that is necessary for continued production but does not itself generate extra shoes. That is, with less than 30 workers doing overhead for uppers, *no* uppers can be produced at that plant. Setting aside more than 30 workers is possible but unnecessary and so it would reduce production. Similarly, if the plant is to manufacture any soles, it will need to set aside a minimum of 30 workers for sole-related overhead.

Now consider the effect of self-sufficiency. After setting aside 60 workers at each plant to enable the factory to produce uppers *and* soles, there are only 240 workers left to do so. Dividing them equally, each plant produces 12,000 sets of uppers and soles, for a company-wide total of 24,000 shoes. Suppose instead that Korea specialized completely in uppers and Thailand in soles. Then 30 workers in each location would be freed from overhead activities to engage in production. The result would be an increase of output to 27,000 shoes. This expansion is a rationalization-based gain from trade. The gain from trade is now a 12.5% increase in productivity (from 40 to 45 shoes per worker per day) rather than the 10% shown for the comparative advantage example. This similarity just reflects the specific numbers I used for productivity and for overhead requirements. The key idea is that "indivisibilities" create a second source of gains from trade—the avoidance of unnecessary duplication of fixed costs. We use the term *rationalization* to describe these gains since wasteful overhead costs are eliminated by concentrating a given activity in a smaller number of locations.

This fundamental source of gains from trade here are *returns to scale*. The phenomenon is actually broader than it appears. We could have obtained the same result by assuming that each factory that wants to make uppers must spend a fixed amount on a leather cutting machine and each sole-making factor needs a rubber molding machine. Put another way, the basis for gains to trade from returns to scale is a decline in average costs of an activity whenever output in a specific location increases. Whenever average costs of production for a plant are decreasing in the amount currently produced at that plant, we will say that there are *plant-level economies of scale* (PLEoS).

The two main causes of PLEoS are indivisible inputs (like the overhead workers we have already considered) and geometric relationships between cost and capacity. Geometric PLEoS usually arise from surface-volume relationships. Consider the following example. Beer is made in cylindrical vats. The cost of the steel used in the vat is roughly proportional to its surface area, that is $K = 2c\pi rh + 2c\pi r^2$, where c is the cost per square meter of the steel, r is the vat's radius, and h is the vat's height. The quantity of beer produced is equal to the volume of the vat: $Q = \pi r^2 h$. Average costs are given by the cost of ingredients (malt, hops) and labour per liter plus average capital costs per liter. The latter are given by $K/Q = 2c(1/h + 1/r)$. For any given volume, the area is minimized when the height is twice the radius. Making substitutions, $K/Q = 3c/r$. This means that average costs can be reduced when you use larger vats. Rewriting K/Q in terms of quantity, some algebra shows that

$$\frac{K}{Q} = \frac{3c(2\pi)^{1/3}}{Q^{1/3}}.$$

This expression gives us an important lesson. Average cost curves can be downward sloping even if there are no costs that are entirely fixed, i.e. no indivisibilities. The geometric PLEoS occur whenever capital

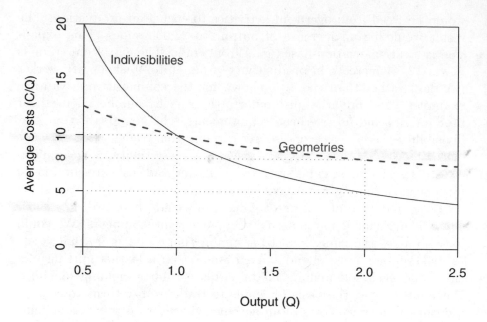

Fig. 2.2. Plant-level economies of scale

costs depend on area and output depends on volume. This will be the case whenever production involves some type of container, such as a furnace, kiln, kettle, pipe, or tank. Geometric scale economies are therefore also important in the chemical, steel-making, aircraft assembly industries.

Figure 2.2 illustrates the two sources of PLEoS. The solid line (intersecting the vertical axis at 20) shows how average costs fall when there are indivisible fixed costs. In that case average capital costs are F/Q. The dashed line corresponds to the case of production using a cylinder. These average costs exclude other variable inputs like production workers and raw materials and can be thought as showing average capital costs under two scenarios. I selected the numerical values of F and c so that the curves would intersect at an output level shown as 1.0 (an arbitrary unit scale that could be measured in grams, kilos, tons, etc.). Now suppose a firm is going to produce two units in all. If it uses two separate factories, the average capital cost at each is 10. However, by concentrating production in a single factory, it can lower average costs by 50% (to 5) in the case of PLEoS derived from indivisibilities and by 20% (to 8) with PLEoS derived from geometries. The reason why the gains are not as large with geometries is that producing more output in a location requires more capital (a bigger vat). However, the capital in use does not have to increase as much as the increase in output because surface areas of cylinders rise less rapidly than their volumes.

In addition to static PLEoS, gains from trade can also arise from plant-specific learning-by-doing. This effect (also known as *dynamic scale economies* or the *experience curve*) is important in many industries such as aircraft, semiconductors, steel, and televisions. The basic idea is that the more *cumulative* output is manufactured in a plant, the better "calibrated" will be the workers and equipment to efficient production. In learning that is plant-specific, the series of small adjustments to the production process do not result in transferable process technologies because they are *tacit* (not codified and therefore nearly impossible to communicate) therefore remain localized within the plant where the learning occurred.

One rather special feature of gains to trade from returns to scale is that it does not matter at all which country specializes in what. Indeed, in the long run, when labour contracts terminate, *any* difference in wages would cause the firm to close the factory in the high wage country and produce both soles and uppers in the low wage factory. In contrast, we showed that under comparative advantage, there is a wide band of relative wages in which each country specializes in one activity and this activity has to be the one in which they have lower opportunity costs.

References

The numerical comparative advantage problem that this chapter revolves around was inspired by the treatment in Brander's textbook. For a more standard and thorough treatment of comparative advantage and gains from trade, see an international economics textbook, such as Krugman and Obstfeld. The Haldi and Whitcomb article below is an old, but useful, account of the underpinnings and magnitudes of plant level economies of scale.

Brander, James, 1995 *Government Policy Towards Business*, Third edition, Wiley, Toronto.

Haldi, John and David Whitcomb, 1967, "Economies of Scale in Industrial Plants" *The Journal of Political Economy*, 75(4), 373–385.

Krugman, Paul and Maurice Obstfeld, *International Economics: Theory and Policy*, Sixth edition, Addison Wesley.

3

Factor Advantages

In the previous chapter we used the international shoe production example to explore the issue of how to find the best location for each activity required for creating a final product. Another way to phrase the question is to ask what goods and services should each country export and which ones should it import from its trading partners?

The obvious solution is for me to export to you the things that I am good at making and that you are poor at making. Ricardo realized that I could be worse than you (as measured by productivity) in every activity but nevertheless I could still export to you the things that I am *relatively less bad* at, i.e. those things in which I have a comparative advantage.

The problem with the basic Ricardian analysis is that it does not yet provide a satisfying answer to our questions. For instance, Canada is one of the world's largest suppliers of newsprint. Why? Well, because it has a comparative advantage in newsprint production. But why? Relative to other nations, Canada has a lower opportunity cost of devoting resources to making newsprint. But *why*? In this chapter we argue that locations have comparative advantage—and in equilibrium, competitive advantage as well—in making products that use locally abundant factors of production. We will refer to competitive advantages derived from the quality or quantity of local factors as *factor advantages*.

3.1 Factor Abundance

Two Swedish economists, Heckscher and Ohlin, provided an account of the source of comparative advantage which has become the standard explanation. Their *Factor Proportions Theory* predicts that countries will be *net exporters of products that use their relatively abundant factors intensively*. This definition is pretty dense in terminology which must be defined carefully.

Products: tradeable goods and services made from factors and intermediate inputs (products that are used to make other products rather than for final consumption).

Factors: the economic resources which—when combined—create goods. Factors should be distinguished from intermediate inputs. Electricity is not, strictly speaking, a factor. However, the rivers which give a country the capacity to generate hydroelectric power would be, as is also the dam.

There are many different ways to categorize the factors of production but the most common distinction is between labour and capital:

- Labour (L): raw man-power.
- Capital (K): The concept of capital is not just physical capital (plant and equipment). It has been broadened to include human, intellectual, social, and natural capital. A general definition for capital would be an object that delivers a stream of benefits (or "services") over time. To be capital, something must be both useful and durable. When the legal rights to the benefits delivered by capital are assigned to an entity, the capital becomes "property."

We define each form of capital in the list below.

physical capital : manmade tangible objects that provide services for an extended period of time, namely structures and equipment (sometimes referred to as "fixed assets"). When use of physical capital is shared broadly, it is often referred to as "infrastructure." Examples of the latter include fiber optic networks, power transmission grids, highway systems.[1]

intellectual capital : codified knowledge or information (of a kind that is reusable and sellable). It takes the form of sets of instructions, depictions, representations, narrations, identifications. When the owner has exclusive legal use rights, intellectual capital becomes intellectual property. The three main forms of intellectual property are patents (covering depictions and instructions), trademarks (representations and identifications), and copyrights (narrations).

---

[1] The *Economics A-Z* entry defines infrastructure as "Roads, ports, railways, airports, power lines, pipes and wires that enable people, goods, commodities, water, energy and information to move about efficiently."

The intellectual capital possessed by a firm is also referred to as an "intangible asset."

natural capital : objects not created by human activity that can be used over a sustained period by humans. Examples include natural harbours, fertile soil, underground reserves of water, oil, natural gas, and ores. The position of places relative to the equator (latitude) gives access to the heat of the sun in certain valuable ways that may be thought of as natural capital (for the wine industry, for example).

human capital : cognitive abilities acquired through education, training, and experience, also referred to as skills. Human capital is knowledge embodied in people. Human capital is needed to produce intellectual capital and it also is enhanced by intellectual capital. However, human capital (for example, the ability to write a computer program) is conceptually distinct from intellectual capital (for example, a computer program) because human capital resides in individual human brains, whereas intellectual capital is codified.

social capital : linkages between people that facilitate cooperation (mutual trust, adherence to civic norms, and membership in associations). For social capital to exist, there must be at least two actors. (Thus, the fictional castaway, Robinson Crusoe, had his own human capital on the island, but he had no social capital until the arrival of his helper, Friday.) In addition, there must be at least some common interest: rivals do not have social capital.

The key idea of Factor Advantages is a *matching* process. A location is a good match for an activity if it has a relative abundance in the factors used relatively intensively by the activity. Relative *abundance* can be defined using ratios or shares. First, when considering just two countries (Home and Foreign) and two factors (capital and labour), we can use the *ratio test*. For example we could compare physical capital per worker in the two countries. We say that the home country (H) has relative abundance of capital (K) compared to the foreign country (F) if

$$\frac{K_H}{L_H} > \frac{K_F}{L_F}.$$

The problem with the ratio test is that the world has more than 200 countries, not just two. Moreover, we have listed many types of capital and, therefore, there are many possible ratios one could calculate. To take into account many factors and countries, we rely on the *share test* which states that a country has relative abundance in some factor if its share of the world's supply of that factor exceeds its share of world

Table 3.1. Factor abundance in three countries

	Canada	US	Japan	World
Factor Supply				
Crop Land, m hec	45.5	187.8	4.5	1465
(as % of world)	3.1%	12.8%	0.3%	100.0%
Pasture Land, m hec	27.9	239.2	0.66	3410
	0.8%	7.0%	0.0%	100.0%
Forest Land, m hec	453	296	25	4177
	10.8%	7.1%	0.6%	100.0%
Water, th km^3	2849.5	2459.1	547	41022
	6.9%	6.0%	1.3%	100.0%
Labour, m	16	136	67	2784
	0.6%	4.9%	2.4%	100.0%
Factor Demand				
GNI, tr US$	0.57	7.1	4.96	27.7
	2.1%	25.6%	17.9%	100.0%

Sources: World Resources Institute for natural endowments and World Bank for labour force statistics.

income. We will follow the convention among economists and use Y to represent a country's gross national income (GNI). Home has relative abundance (according to the share test) in K if

$$\frac{K_H}{K_W} > \frac{Y_H}{Y_W}.$$

Table 3.1 shows absolute abundance of four factors in three countries. It also provides the GNI information needed to calculate shares tests. We see that the US has absolute abundance in crop land relative to Canada and Japan. However by the shares test, Canada is relatively abundant in crop land whereas the US and Japan are relatively scarce. Using crop land relative to labour, the ratio test shows us that both Canada and the US are relatively abundant in crop land as compared to Japan.

A factor is used *intensively* in production of a good if it accounts for a high share of the cost of producing that good. Table 3.2 provides the type of data one would use to measure factor intensity. We consider a

Table 3.2. Factor intensity in various manufacturing industries

Industry (NAICS)	$(I+P)/V$	L/V	H/V	H/L
Telephony (33421)	32.5%	30.2%	37.3%	1.23
Footwear(3162)	48.8%	39.0%	12.2%	0.31
Furniture (3371)	52.5%	38.1%	9.4%	0.25
All Manufacturing (31-33)	61.9%	27.9%	10.2%	0.36
Pharmaceuticals (3254)	63.0%	16.2%	20.8%	1.28
Agri-Chemicals (3253)	66.8%	21.4%	11.8%	0.55
Aluminum (3313)	74.5%	21.5%	4.0%	0.19
Petroleum Refining (32411)	88.5%	7.2%	4.3%	0.60

Note: L, and H are expenditures on production workers and administrative employees. V is value-added. $I+P$ (intellectual and physical capital) is calculated as the $V-L-H$. H/L is a proxy for the skill intensity of the workforce.
Source: ⟨strategis.ic.gc.ca ⟩

product to be intensive in a factor if the cost share of that factor in the industry is higher than the average. Thus, we can see the capital intensity of the petroleum manufacturing manifested in its 88.5% cost share for intellectual and physical capital (relative to 62% for the average industry). Conversely the labour intensity of footwear is evident in its production labour share of 39% (relative to 28%). One important practical question is how to handle material inputs. Indirectly they embody factor services.

So why do we export newsprint? Because newsprint makes intensive use of two factors "forest land" and "capital" that are relatively abundant in Canada. And why do we export aluminum? Again, because of the relative abundance of the resources used to generate power, the most important factor in manufacturing aluminum.

Why is Hollywood the largest producer of movies? A hard-core advocate of factor proportions theory would argue that the climate there was important in allowing movies to be filmed outdoors year-around, something that could not be done in most other places. There is some doubt whether this argument has much empirical relevance. When the industry was established, most movies were filmed indoors in studios. More persuasive explanations for the Hollywood phenomenon will draw on ideas of Michael Porter presented later in this chapter.

Why do we import clothing from China? Because China has a relatively abundant supply of low-skilled labour used intensively in clothing production. Note if 50% of China's work force had college degrees, they would still have an absolute abundance in low-skilled labour but they would no longer have a relative abundance.

Physical and intellectual capital are created by individual decisions not to consume all the income they generate, but rather to save some of it. This generates the pool of loanable funds that ultimately becomes the physical stock of plant and equipment. It also contributes to the creation of patented inventions. The sets of contractual claims on the returns (dividends and interest) generated by the physical and intellectual capital possessed by a corporation can be referred to as financial capital. The two chief forms of financial capital are stocks and bonds (equity and debt securities). Financial capital is highly mobile, both in its portfolio form (mutual fund investments, bond holdings) and in "direct" form (multinational enterprises). However, studies have shown that most of what people save is invested locally. Across a sample of nations, savings rates and investment rates are highly correlated. This suggests a country's savings may indeed be seen as an "endowment" of capital.

3.2 The Case of Cashmere

Cashmere has been considered a luxurious fabric since the time of the Roman Empire.[2] In 1999, an increase in supply combined with a decrease in Japanese demand generated unusually low prices and high availability for cashmere in US stores. The cashmere sweater business involves the following steps:

1. *Raise goats* that grow a "fine, downy undercoat as a defense against the bitter cold." Raw cashmere is produced in just four countries: China (60%), Mongolia, Afghanistan and Iran (small amounts). "Scottish" and "Italian" cashmere are actually just spinning, knitting and weaving operations.
2. *Comb* out the cashmere in the spring. Using a large, wide-toothed metal comb, the farmer tugs out the so-called "greasy cashmere" which—in addition to the cashmere down—contains coarse hair, dirt, and vegetation.
3. *Sort* the greasy cashmere by color. White is most valuable because it can be dyed any other color.
4. *Dehair:* Using simple machines, separate the down from other matter (hair, dirt, etc.).

---

[2] This subsection draws extensively on Rebecca Mead's February 1, 1999 article in *The New Yorker*, called "The Crisis in Cashmere."

5. *Inspect:* How long is the down? Longer fibres are the best.
6. *Spin* the fluffy down into yarn or thread.
7. *Dye* the yarn the appropriate color.
8. *Weave* the yarn into bolts of fabric.
9. *Design* clothing items that use the cashmere.
10. *Sew* the fabric into sweaters, shawls, etc.
11. *Distribute* the clothing to retail stores like Banana Republic, Neiman Marcus, Club Monaco.

Factor abundance is an important determinant of where each activity takes place. Perhaps most importantly, the goats must be raised in cold climates which is what causes the goats to grow the wool used in cashmere. Combing must be done where the goats are, of course. Sorting and dehairing are low-skill activities and hence also appropriate for China and Mongolia. Doing these activities near where the goats are raised also lowers transport costs since the extracted fibres are lighter and less voluminous than the raw bunches of hair. Spinning, dyeing and weaving are done in many places such as the US, UK, and Italy. Design of the products occurs in fashion centers such as Milan and New York City.

3.3 Factor Quality

Management strategy professor Michael Porter criticized "factor-driven" theories of trade. Porter proposed instead that innovation, not relative factor abundance, was the key to obtaining competitive advantage. His 1990 book, *The Competitive Advantage of Nations* drew on numerous case studies of successful national industries.

Rather than pointing to expenditures on R&D or the inspiration of brilliant inventors, Porter argues "Innovation is the result of unusual effort." Moreover, "Innovation usually requires pressure, necessity, and even adversity: the fear of loss often proves more powerful than the hope of gain."

Porter argues that factor conditions are important determinants of competitive advantage but in a very different way from the standard trade theory introduced by Heckscher and Ohlin. To make things clearer, consider the following typology of factors.

Factor Proportions Theory focuses on factors of type I (e.g. forest land) and II (e.g. a telecommunications network, or a pool of educated workers). Porter argues that basic and general-use factors do not generate sustained competitive advantage.

Table 3.3. Michael Porter's typology of factors

		Origin	
		Basic (Endowed)	Advanced (Created)
Specificity:	General-use	I	II
	Industry-specific	III	IV

Porter argued that abundance of basic factors may actually undermine competitive advantage. Why?

1. General-use factors are widely available, so it is possible to switch from country to another. Moreover, many innovations are designed to economize on general-use factors such as labour. These forces, Porter argues, make it very difficult to obtain sustained advantage based on abundant general-use factors.
2. Abundance generates waste. Scarcity generates innovative mindset.

One example might be forest-based industries in British Columbia. Lumber has seen rising competition from Chile and the Southeastern United States. The virgin newsprint industry has felt the rise of competition from the "urban forest"—recycled newspaper.[3]

Porter's prime example of competitive advantage based on innovation is the fresh-cut flower industry of Holland ($1 billion in annual exports). Despite an inhospitable climate (cold and sunless winters), Dutch flower growers innovated in the areas of glass-house growing and energy conservation (they took advantage of abundant natural gas).

We may define selective factor disadvantage (SFD) as the absence of a basic factor that would be advantageous to have in abundance if there were no dynamic effects. An SFD can stimulate innovation which more than compensates for the original disadvantage. SFDs are best when they send an accurate signal about circumstances that will ultimately prevail elsewhere. Since resource depletion seems to be a general trend, it pays to be the first mover in figuring out how to generate more output with fewer resources.

---

[3] Nevertheless, forest-products are a huge export for BC, and give us a clear example of the benefits of factor abundance. Perhaps we are not as competitive as we might be, but the "curse of abundance" was not so strong as to actually cause the loss of comparative advantage in the industry.

Examples of SFDs:

- Switzerland: first country to experience labour shortage. Abandoned labour-intensive watches and concentrated on innovative and/or high-end watches (Rolex, Swatch).
- Japan: high priced land led to a high cost of factory space which led to development of the J.I.T. system.
- Sweden: A short building season plus high construction costs led to development of pre-fabricated housing.

Rather than basic general-use factors, Porter claims that *advanced, specialized factors that are man-made (type IV) are harder to imitate and therefore more valuable.*

Examples of type IV factors include UC Davis's enology and viticulture programs that benefit the Napa and Sonoma wine regions, Denmark's hospitals that benefit the country's insulin producers, and Dutch banks that accept flower bulbs as collateral. Also the Dutch flower industry benefits from highly specialized research centers on cultivation, packaging, shipping (refrigerated so it blooms in shop). Venture capital houses that cater to specific industries (biotechnology, oil, entertainment, software) are increasing their importance relative to "generalists."

Why are specialized factors harder to imitate? Porter does not offer a clear answer. One hypothesis is that scale effects in the provision of such factors lead to a Catch 22 for new entrants. Specialized factors are unavailable locally because the industry is too small to justify investments in factor creation. But the local industry is small because of poor local factor conditions.

While Porter's hypothesis is intriguing, we should note that there are many cases where abundance of general-use factors appear to generate comparative advantage:

- Canadian hydroelectric generating potential: strength in energy-intensive goods like aluminum.
- Argentinean pasture land leads to exports of leather.
- Japanese workers who are skilled at assembling a variety of complex products: exports of cars and consumer electronics.
- US innovation-based industries such as pharmaceuticals and biotechnology draw on general US strength in basic (university) science.

My view is that Heckscher and Ohlin are right that factor abundance is usually a source of competitive advantage for a country and not an impediment as Porter argues. Factor abundance is good for industries that use a factor intensively. While factor scarcity might have some off-setting properties, like the inducement to innovate, a firm would still benefit from producing where it can obtain its inputs cheaply. British Columbia's sawmills should not relocate to the deserts of Arizona just because this would force them to think up innovative solutions for how to obtain logs. Despite these criticisms, Porter does make some valid points. He is right to emphasize that many important factors are created rather than endowed by nature. He is also right that many factors are not general-use. Furthermore, it is obvious that the quality of factors should be considered, rather than just raw quantities. Nevertheless, none of the correct ideas in Porter truly contradict the standard theory: producers of a good should prefer—other things equal—locations where intensively used factors are available at low cost (relative to their quality).

3.4 Dynamics of Comparative Advantage

Comparative advantage can change dramatically over time. What a country once exported in large quantities, it may later mainly import. Back in 1966, Raymond Vernon proposed that many products appear to follow a similar pattern—called the international product life cycle (IPLC)—in terms of the temporal evolution of where they are produced and consumed.

New products are manufactured and consumed in the "inventing country." Initially the inventing firm(s) produce and sell the product exclusively at home. Later, the inventing country starts to export to other countries, which will initially also be advanced (high income) countries.

Maturing products experience spread of production to other advanced countries. The inventing country gradually loses those countries as export markets.

Standardized product begin to be manufactured in less developed countries. The inventing country becomes an importer. Consumption in the inventing country begins to decline as new inventions attract consumers.

Figure 3.1 adapts a figure from page 199 of Vernon's (1966) article. The top frame shows the rise and subsequent decline of production in the inventing country. Here I've intentionally modified Vernon's figure which designated the US as the sole inventing country. Vernon considered the United States to be the primary source of inventions because

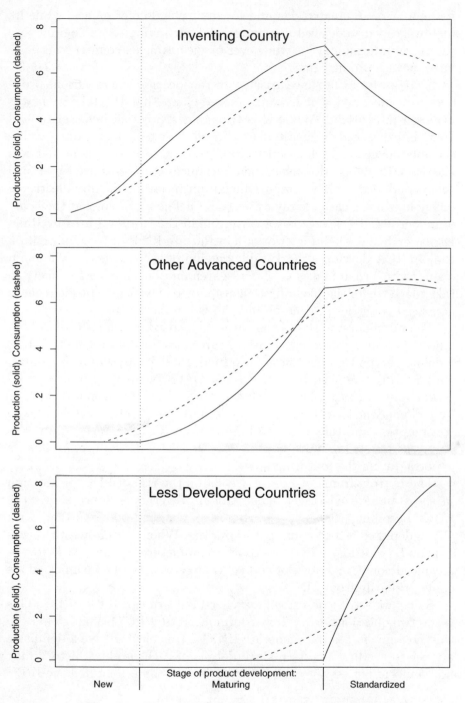

Fig. 3.1. Vernon's international product life-cycle

its high incomes created demand for luxury and convenience, while its high wages led to derived demand for labour-saving technologies. Here the "inventing country" is whichever of the advanced countries actually introduced a product first.

Endless arguments have arisen over the location where various products were invented. For example, some claim that the television was invented in Scotland. While it is true that a Scottish inventer named John Baird is widely credited as the "first person to produce a discernible image on a television screen,"[4] his laboratory was actually in Hastings, England. Moreover, the mechanical apparatus used by Baird was abandoned shortly after its invention in favour of fully electronic technology using cathode ray tubes (CRT). The technology at the heart of modern CRT televisions was invented in the United States by Philo Farnsworth and Vladimir Zworykin in the late 1920s. Zworykin went on to help RCA develop a marketable version of the television. The main claim that Vernon makes is that research and development is likely to take place where the likely first customers for inventions reside, that is advanced countries in general and the US in particular.

The middle frame shows that other advanced countries (OACs) begin by consuming products imported from the inventing country (IC). I define the end of the "new" product stage as the moment (shown with a dotted vertical line) when the OACs begin to produce. OAC production can take place in factories owned by the inventing firm or by independent local firms. Gradually, OAC production catches up to consumption and they cease to import from IC. Due to the rise in demand from less developed countries (LDCs), the IC still maintains its exports during the maturing stage.

The bottom frame of Figure 3.1 shows the rise of LDC production in the standardized stage. This version of Vernon's figure shows the LDCs becoming the dominant world producers and exporters, with OACs depicted as becoming net importers. When Vernon wrote, it was still quite rare for LDCs to export manufactured goods back to the advanced countries. Now, of course, a large variety of consumer goods come primarily from LDCs.

So far we've just described a stylized pattern called the IPLC. This raises two questions. First, how common is the IPLC? Second, what are the economic forces that generate IPLCs? It is hard to give a definitive answer to the first question since details of each product history may not conform perfectly to the IPLC. However, something like the IPLC

---

[4] http://en.wikipedia.org/wiki/John_Logie_Baird

seems to have occurred with products such as sewing machines, washing machines, office machinery, televisions, and video recorders.

There are important exceptions. For example the Barbie doll, invented in 1969 was never produced in the inventing country (the US). Instead Barbie was made initially in Japan which at that time was somewhere in between LDC and OAC status. In other cases, production disperses to OACs but does not go to LDCs in sizeable amounts. This is the case for large commercial aircraft. Another exception is the case where production disperses worldwide but it is mainly to serve local demand with little importing by the IC and OAC from the LDCs. An important example is automobiles. Large LDCs like Brazil and China produce impressive numbers of cars (2.6 and 7.2 million, respectively, in 2006) but sell most of them at home (95% in the case of China).[5]

When Vernon developed his IPLC hypothesis, he framed it as a challenge to traditional models of comparative advantage. I argue here that the traditional model can understand the IPLC if we allow for a few simple modifications. First, the spread of production to other OACs in the maturing stage makes sense since the IC and OACs both tend to be abundant in high-skilled workers and capital, but relatively scarce in low-skilled workers. This means that they are likely to be good at producing the same things. The delay shown in the middle frame could reflect the time it takes for the inventing firm's patents to expire or the time it takes for competitors to reverse-engineer the new product and introduce their own "copy-cat" versions.

The bigger problem is to explain the transition that occurs in the final stage. Under static factor proportions theory, we would expect a product to either be produced in the advanced countries if it is skilled-labour-intensive, or to be produced in the LDCs if it is unskilled-labour-intensive. A partial explanation is that relative factor abundances shifted over time. The inventing country (the U.S. in many cases) loses part of its relative factor abundance in high-skilled workers, while developing nations increase their relative abundance in skilled labor. But the US rank in terms of relative skill abundance has not declined below that of Korea or Taiwan so we cannot explain why products like microwave ovens and televisions are now produced in those countries and imported by the U.S. that way.

One story that shows up in some textbooks is that in the early life of a product, the inventor is a monopolist. Initially the demand for the product is not price-sensitive but then—maybe because of entry of

---

[5] AFX International Focus, January 11, 2007; Associated Press January 10, 2007; CNN/Money online January 1, 2007.

new competitors from the OACs—price starts mattering more so the company moves production to a cheaper place.

There is a big problem with the "competitive pressure" explanation for the IPLC: Cost-minimization is desirable whether demand is price-sensitive or not. If Jakarta is the lowest cost production site, then you should produce there on your own initiative not because you were "forced" to do so. Think about Nike: it has a fairly large degree of market power due to its unique image in the shoe industry. It *could* produce in higher cost locations and pass on (most of) the higher costs to consumers. However, it chooses to seek out the lowest cost locations possible. Another example might be Polaroid which went international for production even though it was still a monopolist on instant cameras. Why? Because even in the absence of competitive pressure, other things equal, firms still can raise their profits by lowering costs. It is the case, however, that when the firms face more elastic demand curves that the gain from reducing marginal costs becomes larger. The upshot is that while firms always have an incentive to lower their costs, the incentive to lower marginal costs is bigger when consumers are more price-sensitive.

A second problem with the competitive pressure story is that it cannot explain why firms from LDCs do not start producing as soon as imitation becomes possible. Why should they delay longer than the firms in the OACs if indeed they have a cost advantage?

There is a better explanation available that can handle both of the above issues. This explanation lies in the name of the third stage: "standardized products." If the standardization is on the production side, it could mean that the techniques of production have changed for the product such that it has become less skill intensive than it was in the new and maturing product stages. I call this the *factor intensity switch*. As a result of learning-by-doing, the production processes are "routinized." Television production was "high technology" in the 1950s, requiring highly skilled workers. By the 1980s, putting together TVs had become "low tech," something that could be carried out with mainly unskilled (low education) workers. This account suggests that once we allow for standardization to transform factor use intensities, factor proportions theory can easily explain IPLCs.

Two additional explanations that do not involve shifting comparative advantage should be mentioned here since they probably contribute as well. The first invokes intra-firm communication costs. Initially a product will require a number of modifications to respond to consumer needs and whims. To be responsive, production must occur near the target market. A second implication points to the urgency of getting products to market and to the entrepreneur's imperfect information. There may be substantial potential demand for a new product. Hence, a key profit concern is to get it into production quickly and start exploiting your temporary monopoly position as soon as possible. So if you invented it in your garage in Palo Alto then that is where you first look to start producing because that is of your local knowledge. If you searched for the ideal production site, you might ultimately find the lowest cost site in the world but you would lose two years of sales to customers who were willing to pay high markups anyway. So, this story says it was always your intention to add capacity later in low cost sites. Although it sometimes looks like competition is forcing the move, it is really just delayed cost-minimization.

The main message of this chapter is that a country that has the right factors of production in relative abundance at the right time for a product will usually obtain competitive advantage in making that product.

References

Porter, Michael, "The Competitive Advantage of Nations," *Harvard Business Review* 1991.

Torres, Alberto, 1999, "Unlocking the value of intellectual assets." McKinsey Quarterly No. 4, pp. 28–37.

Vernon, Raymond, 1966, "International Investment and International Trade in the Product Cycle," *The Quarterly Journal of Economics*, 80(2), 190–207.

4

Trade Costs

The comparative advantages and scale economies described in Chapter 2 provide us with powerful gains from trade. That is they suggest why it is foolish to try to achieve economic self-sufficiency for either individual firms or economies as a whole. However, our discussion so far has neglected the existence of *costs* of trade. In this chapter we discuss how the gains from trade *net* of trade costs tend to decrease whenever a firm exports across national borders and over large distances. Sufficiently large distances and/or border impediments may wipe out entirely the potential gains from trade due to exploiting comparative advantage.

Trade costs fall into four main categories: transport costs (the costs of moving goods across distances), travel/communication costs (especially important for services), trade policy costs (protectionism), and the transaction costs associated with the process of buying and selling. Transport, travel, and communication costs depend on distance. Trade policy costs operate at national borders. Transaction costs can have distance and border components.

4.1 Physical Separation and the Distance Effect

Transporting goods across the globe is inherently costly for five reasons. First, it takes fuel to transport any object. Second, goods are transported in "vessels"—ships, trucks, railcars, pipelines, which are costly to build and operate. Third, all modes of transport require complementary infrastructure: berths and gantries, highways, and rails. Fourth, goods in motion are exposed to a variety of risks, including temperature control, mishandling, storms, and even piracy. Finally, transportation takes time and delay is increasingly viewed by buyers as a serious problem. Fuel, risks, and delay costs are all closely related to distance traveled. Since vessels are capital goods, there is an opportunity cost of tying them up for a period of time, implying another cost for long distance transport. These considerations all suggest that trade costs are an increasing function of distance. Reasoning one step further, we should expect greater distance to lower the net gains from trade and therefore bilateral trade volumes should be negatively related to distance between country pairs. As we shall see the data strongly confirm this expectation.

In 1687, Newton proposed the "Law of Universal Gravitation." It held that the attractive force between two objects i and j is given by the product of the two masses divided by the square of the distance between them. In 1962 Dutch economist Jan Tinbergen proposed that roughly the same functional form could be applied to international trade flows. Indeed, it has since been applied to a whole range of what we might call "social interactions" including migration, tourism, and foreign direct investment. This general gravity law for social interaction may be expressed in roughly the same way as Newton's Law[1]:

$$F_{ij} = G \frac{M_i M_j}{D_{ij}}, \tag{4.1}$$

where notation is defined as follows

- F_{ij} is the "flow" from origin i to destination j, or, in some cases, it represents total volume of interactions between i and j (i.e. the sum of the flows in both directions).
- M_i and M_j are the relevant economic sizes of the two locations.
- D_{ij} is the distance between the locations.
- G is the "gravitational constant." Empirical research has shown that G is not constant at all and depends on such things as free trade agreements, colonial histories, and common languages.

Most trade economists think of gravity as a kind of short-hand representation of supply and demand forces. If country i is the origin, then M_i represents the amount it is willing to *supply*. Meanwhile M_j represents the amount destination j *demands*. The economic sizes of the exporting and importing countries, M_i and M_j, are usually measured with gross domestic product. Finally distance acts as a sort of tax "wedge," imposing trade costs, and resulting in lower equilibrium

---

[1] The main difference from Newton's law is that trade is inversely proportionate to distance whereas gravitational force is inversely proportionate to distance squared.

trade flows. Distance is usually measured as the great circle (as the bird flies) distance from capitol to capitol. For example the distance between France and Germany would be given by the distance between Paris and Berlin.

Even for air travel, great circle distances probably underestimate true distances since they do not take into account that most flights avoid the North Pole. For maritime travel, they do not take into account indirect routes mandated by land barriers. Furthermore international shipping cartels often set freight costs that bear little relationship to distance travelled. Also, the costs of packaging, loading and unloading, seem to be primarily fixed costs that do not vary with distance. Finally center-to-center distances can be quite misleading for nearby countries. Take Canada and the US as a particularly troublesome example. Most studies measure their distance as the approximately 500 miles between Toronto and Chicago. However, goods coming to and from California must travel considerably longer distances. Moreover, the large volume of auto-related trade between Detroit and Windsor takes place over much shorter distances. Taken together, these considerations suggest that center-to-center great circle distances might have a rather weak relationship with trade.

Nevertheless, while there are many reasons to think that great circle distance is a crude measure of underlying physical transport costs, the fact is that distance dramatically lowers trade. With Anne-Celia Disdier, I have collected over 1000 estimates of the effect of distance on trade. Our results show that the inverse distance rule assumed in the trade gravity equation above works remarkably well. This means that *a doubling of distance will decrease trade by one half.*

Leamer and Levinsohn's (1994) survey of the empirical evidence on international trade offers the identification of distance effects on bilateral trade as one of the "clearest and most robust empirical findings in economics." As they point out, the result may seem abstract or even improbable unless one views an actual graph of the data. In Figure 4.1 we can see that we can observe a clear dependence of exports on distance for the exports of two Canadian provinces as well as inter-state trade of two States. Indeed the inverse proportionality to distance works remarkably well for Ontario and California.

4.1.1 Freight Costs

The most obvious reason why distance is costly is because of "freight costs", the amount one must pay a "carrier" (ship, truck, plane) to transport goods. Figure 4.2 shows the relationship between the cost of

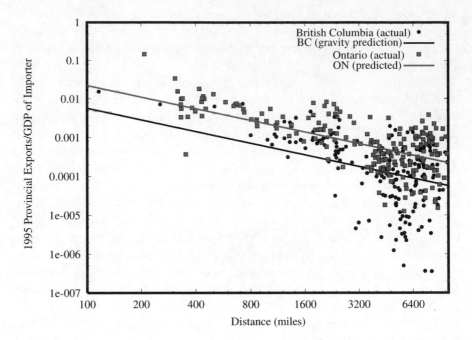

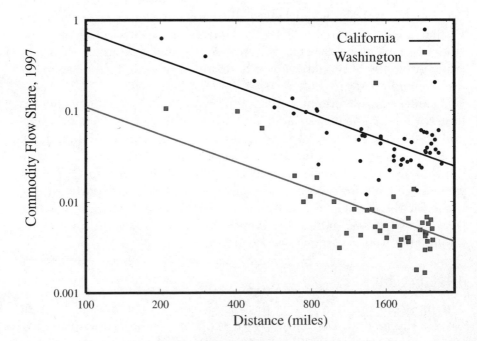

Fig. 4.1. Trade is inversely proportionate to distance

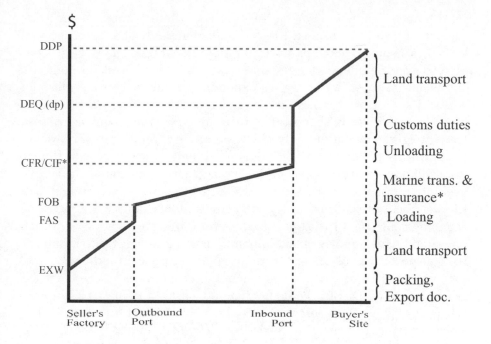

Fig. 4.2. Distance and border related direct trade costs

delivering a good to various locations. The figure also introduces the International Commercial (INCO) terms that every exporter and importer should be familiar with. These terms are defined and elaborated on in this chapter's appendix.

There are a few notable cases where the physical costs of moving goods across space are so high that profitable transactions are impossible, except perhaps over very short distances. Examples include skyscrapers, ready-mix concrete, and the molten pig iron emerging from a blast furnace. For the most part, however, transport costs do not pose an insurmountable barrier to trade.

Hummels (1999) finds that "transport costs pose a barrier at least as large, and frequently larger than tariffs."[2] His study of import data from the US, New Zealand, and five Latin American nations in 1994 revealed that total expenditures on freight range from 4 to 13 percent of the value of imports.

---

[2] David Hummels, "Have International Transportation Costs Declined?" University of Chicago manuscript, September 1999 describing "Toward a Geography of Trade Costs", a January 1999 manuscript.

Hummels points out several reasons why these numbers *understate* the actual cost of transport. First, they include only the "international leg" of transport, excluding port and inland charges. It may be reasonable to exclude inland charges since these would be born on domestic shipments anyway. However, port expenditures can be considerable and add to the cost of international purchases.

A second issue is that aggregate freight rates are equivalent to a trade-weighted average of individual commodity freight rates. However, trade will tend to be small on items with high transport costs. Hence, they will receive little weight in the average. Hummels found the simple average (unweighted) of freight rates is two to three times higher than the weighted rates. Consider the following simple example. Suppose the economy consists of two equal sized sectors. In a free trade world each one would have imports of 200 billion dollars. However, trade is subject to transport costs of 2% of the value goods shipped in industry 1 and 10% in industry 2. On average, then the economy is affected by 6% transport costs. Due to the high transport costs in industry 2, imports fall from 200 to 50, whereas they only fall to 150 in industry 1. The weighted average transport costs are 4%, which underestimates their actual importance.

Limao and Venables' (2000) study examined the cost of transporting a 40 foot container from Baltimore to 64 different foreign destinations. They included the overland segment of transportation (if any) to reach the destination city. Their regression analysis found that each kilometer of sea distance added nineteen cents ($0.19) to freight costs, whereas land distance was more expensive, costing $1.38 per km. These costs were in addition to a constant cost averaging $2060 per container and an additional $2017 for reaching landlocked destinations.

4.1.2 Time Costs

While ocean shipping has traditionally been the primary means of transporting goods from one nation to another the role of air shipping has increased markedly. The United States, for instance now receives 30% of its imports by air in comparison with 7% in 1965 and near zero in 1950. According to Hummels (2000), air freight for US trade in 1998 was "seven times more expensive than ocean freight for comparable goods and routes." The obvious reason why firms are willing to pay such a high premium is to save on time in transit. "Shipping containers from European ports to the US Midwest requires 2-3 weeks; Far Eastern ports as long as 6 weeks. In contrast, air shipping requires only a day or less to most destinations." Hummels may be underestimating air travel times, which can take 2–4 days from Asia (or even Europe) to North America. The reason is that direct flights are rare and air cargo is even more likely than human travelers to miss connections and wait around before finally being transferred. Moreover, certain sea routes are considerably faster than six weeks. For instance, some importers report that shipping time from Hong Kong to Los Angeles could take as little as eleven days.

Time in transit is costly for a variety of reasons. The simplest but probably least important reason is the opportunity cost of tying up valuable goods in a kind of "floating inventory." These costs are given by the value of the goods multiplied by the annual interest rate multiplied by the fraction of the year it takes the goods to arrive. However, doing the calculation for a typical 3 week trip with prevailing interest rates of 7% leads to a "floating inventory" cost of just 0.4% of the goods value. Much more important are time costs that involve the reduction or elimination of the value of the good because it took too long to arrive. We refer to such losses of value caused by delay as the "perishing" of the good. *Perishability* may be interpreted quite broadly to include the following risks:

1. Damage or loss of the good due to weather or mishandling (e.g. ship sinks in a storm). Some but not all sources of damage and loss can be covered by marine *insurance*.
2. Spoilage of organic materials (e.g. maggot infestation of meat, wilting of fresh-cut flowers, loss of efficacy for some types of medicine). Air-tight packaging and refrigerated containers can be deployed to mitigate these costs.
3. Loss of a sale because the good arrives after the date when it was required by the intended purchaser. This is important for time-sensitive goods like newspapers, seasonal goods like Christmas presents, and goods affected by rapidly changing fashions. Note that delay is not the only process at work in these cases. Otherwise, the supplier would simply choose to ship the good with exactly enough lead time to reach the consumer at the required time. This does not work well in the examples mentioned above because each type of good is more valuable if produced soon before it is consumed. Furthermore variability in delivery time is likely to rise with the expected length of the trip.
4. Supply chain bottlenecks. A related problem occurs if the good is to be combined with other inputs and processed further. "The absence of key components can idle an entire assembly plant, which increases the optimal inventory on-hand necessary to accommodate

time variation." (Hummels, 2000). Holding large inventories is not a panacea if there is uncertainty in final demand, the space costs of inventory are large, or if the firm wishes to use just-in-time delivery as part of a quality control mechanism.

4.1.3 Travel and Communication Costs

The service sector now accounts for a large and growing share of world trade. This is somewhat remarkable since many people think of services as inherently nontradable. To resolve this puzzle, we need definitions for both services and trade. Webster's dictionary provides 11 meanings for the noun service, but only 4(a) is appropriate: "a helpful act." While a trade in goods is complete when title to and possession of physical objects changes hands from the seller to the buyer, a trade in services is complete when the seller performs the promised action. In practice many products combine goods and services. For example, restaurants offer both goods (the food and beverages) and services (bringing them to the table and cleaning up afterwards). A digital video disk (DVD) bundles a tangible data storage device (good) with a performance by an actor or musician (service).

We define a good or service to be internationally traded if the residence of the consumer of the product is in a different nation from the residence of the producer. This allows for three modes of trading a service. First, the consumer can make a temporary trip to the home of the provider. Second, the provider can travel to the home of the consumer. Third, the service can be transmitted "remotely" across borders.[3]

For the first two trade modes above, a principal trade cost is the *travel cost* of the consumers or suppliers. Jet travel allowed for a huge reduction in those costs but they are still sufficiently high so as to eliminate most trade in services like restaurants, hair cuts, and routine medical care. Remote trade in services is now possible for most information-intensive (involving text, sound, and images) services such as entertainment, software, architecture, and consulting. The cost of transmitting information over distance will be defined as *communication costs*. Earlier in human history, communication over long distances

---

[3] The General Agreement on Trade in Services recognizes a fourth mode of supply, "commercial presence", namely that a firm based in one country can establish an affiliate in another country to provide the service. Examples would include fast food outlets and bank branches. We will not consider that to be "trade" since it would mean that trade in goods and services would be treated asymmetrically (When I buy a Honda Civic made in Ontario, the value of the sale is not considered a trade flow from Japan to Canada.)

required travel. With the invention of writing, communication over distance could be achieved by moving the message instead of the messenger. However, it still took time and there were significant risks of the message being lost en route. The twentieth century was marked by communication advances such as telephones, televisions, faxes, emails, and teleconferencing that have drastically lowered communication costs. This has made it feasible to export some services—those mainly involving movement of information—without the physical movement of the service performer or beneficiary.

Technological changes are now widening the set of potentially tradeable services. The war in Afghanistan provided a vivid illustration of the possibilities:

> Flying a Predator is much like flying any other aircraft. The pilot has a joystick and rudder pedals, and a full set of instruments. The aircraft takes off and lands on a normal runway, and is equipped with radar, infra-red sensors and video cameras, allowing the pilot to track vehicles and take pictures, even through clouds or at night. What distinguishes the Predator from other aircraft, however, is that the pilot is not on board, but seated in a control centre, many miles away. (*Economist* magazine, "Send in the drones," Nov. 8th, 2001)

Thus in principle, pilots residing in Canada might operate planes flying in Angola. Surgeons can use special gloves that, together with visual monitors, provide enough feedback to conduct a surgical operation remotely. The most cutting edge of these new technologies are what Nicolelis (2000) refers to as Type 2 HBMIs (hybrid brain-machine interfaces). These devices sample brain activity, map it into a three-dimensional action, transmit the signal to a remote robotic arm and then receive visual and tactile feedback. Of course, only in the rather remote future will my favorite barber from Barranquilla shampoo and cut my hair by remote control. However, the trend in technology has been to steadily increase the tradability of services.

4.2 Political Separation and the Border Effect

In the Six Forms of Separation, we identified government policies that restrict inflows of goods as one of the chief impediments to international transactions in goods. These policies are generally exercised by customs agents at national borders. In recent years, these border-implemented

policy barriers to trade have diminished. That has led some to conclude that borders no longer matter. For example, Kenichi Ohmae of
McKinsey asserted in *The Borderless World* that

> "National borders have effectively disappeared and, along with
> them, the economic logic that made them useful lines of demar-
> cation in the first place."

This claim is rather extreme and it is hard to believe that Ohmae
intended it to be taken literally. However, when such statements are not
strongly countered, they have a tendency to be accepted as actual facts,
rather than treated as a kind of rhetorical device to grab attention.
In fact, borders have not disappeared. While they have been almost
costless to pass through in parts of Western Europe, they remain as
significant impediments almost everywhere else.

4.2.1 Estimated Border Effects

In 1995 John McCallum (then an economist at McGill University, he
later became Canada's Minister of Defense) published a paper in the
American Economic Review that took many trade economists by sur-
prise.

McCallum's examination of the trade patterns of Canadian provinces
argued that borders must matter a great deal because the typical Canadian province trades 20 times more with other provinces than with
American states of similar size and distance. Since the Canada-US Free
Trade Agreement was implemented, cross-border trade has grown dramatically (around 60%) so it is reasonable to expect that the impact
of the border on trade would be considerably smaller than what Mc-
Callum estimated using 1988 data.

Perhaps the best way to understand the calculation of border effects is to consider the particular case of Ontario's shipments to British
Columbia (BC) and Washington state. The distances involved are essentially the same: Vancouver is a 3366 km flight from Toronto, whereas
Seattle is slightly closer at 3311 km. Washington state is a larger economy than BC. It has about 50% more residents (about 6 million versus
4 million) and on average they earn 74% more.[4] Taking both numbers
into account, the economic size of BC is just 0.376 of Washington.

---

[4] In 2002, GDP per capita of Washington was $61,000 CAD relative to just $35,000
in BC. Part of the reason US incomes looked so high was the weak Canadian dollar in 2002. The same USD income in 2006 would only be equivalent to $44,000
CAD. Unfortunately, 2002 is the most recent year for which I could obtain inter-
provincial trade flows.

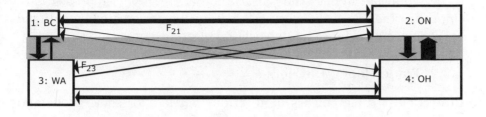

Fig. 4.3. The border effect on Canada-US trade in 2002

These facts are represented in Figure 4.3. The heights of the rectangles representing states and provinces are shown proportional to per capita incomes. The widths are proportional to population. This means areas are proportional to GDPs. The figure is drawn emphasizing the relatively large East-West distances, as compared to North-South distances. The gray bar separating provinces and states represents the Canada-US border.

The gravity equation leads us to expect that Ontario (region 2 in the figure) should export more to Washington (region 3) than BC (region 1). We can calculate the gravity-predicted trade ratio (GPTR) as $(M_1/D_{21})/(M_3/D_{23})$, or, equivalently, $(M_1/M_3)/(D_{21}/D_{23})$. The second expression is relative GDP over relative distance and the intuition behind it is that the gravity model predicts relatively high exports to markets that are relatively *large* (high M_1/M_3) and relatively *proximate* (low D_{21}/D_{23}). In this case, the GPTR is $.376/1.009 = 0.372$.

Washington-bound goods from Ontario must cross a national border. What difference does that make? Even if the border did not matter, the actual trade ratio would not be exactly equal to the GPTR because gravity models applied to human beings are not nearly as exact as gravity models applied to physical objects. However, we would expect F_{21}/F_{23} to be something considerably smaller than one. In the actual 2002 trade data ON exported 5.8 bn to BC and just 1.1 bn to WA, for an actual trade ratio (ATR) of $F_{21}/F_{23} = 5.273$ (illustrated in the figure with a thicker line between ON and BC than the line between ON and WA). We can calculate the border effect for this set of flows as $ATR/GPTR = 5.273/0.372 = 14.2$. *Ontario exports less than one tenth of what it would be predicted to export to Washington in a borderless North American economy.*

Why do borders matter? One approach is to question the methods and the measurements. It is usually a good idea to apply skepticism to statistical results. However, these border effects have been found to be significant in one study after another. A second approach is to emphasize the role of the most visible impediments created by national borders: customs duties and associated clearance procedures.

4.2.2 Trade Policy Barriers

Protectionist trade policies pose serious barriers for some goods and countries. As will be discussed in chapter 5, round after round of multilateral and bilateral tariff reductions, have reduced customs duties substantially for most commodities entering most developed countries. Important exceptions (cheese entering Canada, sugar entering the US) remain but it seems unlikely that the costs of clearing customs explain the estimated effects of borders on trade. It is true that as Canada-US tariffs fell, so also did the estimated impact of the border. This showed that removing even fairly low tariffs (5–10%) could stimulate large increases in trade. However, the border effect remained too large to be explicable in terms of the small remaining trade impediments associated with clearing customs. Another aspect of the Canada-US border that has continued to be important is the difference in currencies.

4.2.3 Currency Conversion Costs

Prior to the implementation of the EURO in January 1999, every large country in the world used its own form of currency. This meant that international business differed from purely domestic trade because of the need to convert payments from one currency to another. How big a cost currency conversion imposes on international business is not clear. First of all there are fees charged by intermediaries, such as banks. While conversion fees are annoying for tourists, the fees charged by banks for large transactions are less than a percent. A second cost imposed by exchange rates is the uncertainty of home currency value of a payable or receivable denominated in foreign currency. Most currencies are highly volatile and might move considerably over a 90 day window. In many cases, however, this risk can be eliminated by selling or buying currency in *forward markets*. These exchange markets connect buyers who need a specific foreign currency at a specific time with sellers who are in the opposite position. This allows them to lock into the exchange rate now, rather than having to worry about changes that occur after making the deal but before consummation.

In the lead-up to the introduction of the Euro, *The Economist* (2001) argued that a world of multiple currencies imposes an additional cost: obscuring price differences. "In the past, manufacturers have been able to maintain price differentials because their customers found it difficult to compare prices." With the Euro, consumers would take advantage of greater "price transparency" to buy from the cheapest source. I find it very hard to believe that this effect is quantitatively important. It seems to hinge on the view that consumers are sophisticated enough to locate identical products in two different countries and costlessly transport the goods from market to market, yet not smart enough to carry out a simple multiplication required to express their prices in a common currency.

While currency conversion costs seem fairly small, there is some evidence from trade patterns that they could be important in practice. A series of papers, mainly by Andrew Rose and co-authors, have found that countries that use the same currency, trade about twice as much with each other as other pairs of otherwise similar countries. Many economists are skeptical of these results and the early evidence for trade with the Euro region does not support such large impacts. A more reasonable estimate is that using a common currency increases trade by about a third.

Trade policies and currency conversion costs probably cannot explain large estimated border effects on their own. In addition to these formal aspects of borders, many economists point to the importance of social and business networks that are much stronger within national borders than across them.

4.3 Relational Separation and Transaction Costs

Transaction costs are the costs incurred during the process of buying or selling. They derive from the fact that the buyer and seller are different entities, each possessing its own private information and incentives. Our definition excludes the costs of production, transportation, and taxation. Thus, it excludes all costs that would be incurred if the provider and user of the goods were a single entity.

Discussions of transaction costs have a tendency towards vagueness. Table 4.1 provides an "anatomy" of transaction costs based on the timing of key events and the sequence of phases in the development of a transaction.

A key problem for importers and exporters is to ensure that goods are delivered (at the promised time, quantity, and quality) and the goods are paid for (at the promised time and the agreed upon amount and form of payment). This is a problem for buyers and sellers even

Table 4.1. Making SENSE of transactions

Event Phase	Activities
1: Buyer demands, Seller offers	
Search	Multilateral learning
	Advertise
	Internet search
2: Buyer/Seller pair meet	
Engage	Bilateral learning
	Inspect seller's samples
	Visit manufacturer's factory
	Check buyer's credit record
	Develop personal
	relationships (*guan xi*)
	Request references
3: Decision to sign contract	
Negotiate Agree on terms	
	product specs, price &quantity
	delivery place & time
	payment form & time
4: Contract signed	
Safeguard Precautions (pre-breach)	
	Payment intermediaries (L/C, PayPal, escrow)
	Insure against non-payment
	Facilitation payments to officials ("grease")
	Hire security for carrier
5: Completion dates (payment & delivery)	
Enforce	Remedies (post-breach)
	Collection agencies
	Mediation
	Courts
	Insurance claims

when they are from the same country but it is exacerbated in international trade by distance (physical and cultural) and by poorly developed enforcement of contracts. What makes international contracts more problematic?

1. At least one party must incur *travel* costs to appear before the foreign court.
2. At least one party must *learn* how a foreign legal system works.

3. Judges and juries may have a *bias* against the foreign party.

Agreements between buyers and sellers are more costly to specify and enforce when the parties reside in different countries. Transaction contracts comprise two promises. First, the seller promises to deliver a specified good, service, or asset at a specified time and place. Second, the buyer promises to pay by a specified time in a specified currency. If either party does not trust the other, opportunities for mutual gains from trade may be foregone. And often the parties will only agree to trade once they have undertaken "defensive" expenditures (credit and/or reference checks, insistence upon bank or government payment guarantees, hiring of inspectors, insurance). Thus, rather than focusing all resources on creating value, the parties divert resources towards reducing the risks of contract breach.

Within networks of buyers and sellers that are all familiar with each other, the concern for maintaining one's reputation is a force which can compel compliance to contracts (even ones that are implicit and signed only with a verbal promise and a handshake). People who breach contracts can be put on literal or figurative "blacklists" which cause them to be shunned by other members of the network. This does not work as well internationally because of the greater anonymity and because reputation-monitoring institutions (eg credit-rating agencies) are mostly absent at the international level.

"You can not fax a handshake," points out one recent television commercial extolling the virtues of airline travel. As a result, before large business transactions, the parties involved often expend substantial amounts of time and money on getting to know each other and building mutual trust.

Problems associated with mistrust exist, of course, in domestic business. Indeed they are the source of institutions such as warranties and credit rating agencies. In the international context, the mistrust problem is severe enough that it has generated a distinctive payment institution: the Letter of Credit.

There are several options for payment. The ones we are most familiar with in a domestic context are also located at the two extremes of whether the buyer or the seller bears the risk associated with imperfect partner information.

Cash in Advance: The buyer pays at the time he orders the product. Then, the seller is supposed to deliver.

Open Account: The seller delivers the product after the buyer orders it. The buyer is supposed to pay within an agreed upon time, e.g. 90 days.

An intermediate approach resembles the "cash on delivery" (COD) payment system sometimes used for domestic transactions. In this case the buyer pays an agent of the seller at the moment the title to the goods changes hands. With trade over large distances, this requires the seller to have an agent who retains title of the good in the foreign country until payment is made. For this reason in international trade this type of transaction is called "documents upon payment" or D/P. The D/P transaction prevents the buyer from obtaining the goods without paying for them. However, it still leaves the risk to the seller that he might transport the goods to the foreign country and then the buyer might not turn up to make payment. One reason is that during the period of shipment, the buyer went bankrupt and is unable to pay. Alternatively, the buyer might have opted to go with a cheaper source. This puts the seller in the difficult position of trying to find another buyer in an unfamiliar location or shipping the goods back home at his own expense. This suggests the need for a better payment institution.

A more attractive solution to the problem of lack of trust between trading partners has been found in the institution of the "Letter of Credit" (abbreviated L/C). The actual practices involved with L/C are complex but we can simplify them down to the following key steps:

1. The buyer goes to his bank and secures a "letter" in which the bank promises to pay for goods upon delivery of certain documents.
2. The seller receives the letter and ships the goods.
3. The shipper (or carrier) completes the trip and presents the stipulated documents to the bank. The most important of these is the "bill of lading" which will turn over ownership of the goods to the buyer.
4. The bank pays the seller.

Note that the problem of distrust is mostly resolved. The seller cannot get paid without delivering the goods. The buyer cannot obtain the goods without making payment. Furthermore, even if during the shipping period, the buyer has decided it does not want to or cannot afford to make the purchase, the bank is still obligated to pay.

Essentially, the L/C substitutes trust in an intermediary, the established bank, for trust in the actual buyer and seller of the good. The bank cares about its reputation because that is the primary service it sells. Meanwhile the banks have better information and enforcement capabilities with respect to home country firms than do foreign firms.

The letter of credit does not, however, provide a complete solution to the lack of trust problem:

1. The L/C is a costly device. The exact amount varies and depends
   in part on the size of the transaction. One former student (Lyle
   Herstein, MBA 2000) reports "At the company I worked for our
   transactions ranged from $100,000.00 to several million and L/C
   charges (excluding flat fee, handling, documentation, and drawing
   charges) were less than 1/4%."
2. The L/C is only valuable if the bank is trustworthy. Sometimes it
   may make sense to involve a home country bank as well that can
   establish the creditworthiness of the foreign bank.
3. The bank can only verify documents. This puts the buyer at risks
   that the documentation will look fine to the bank but the good will
   nevertheless be faulty in some way; for instance the freight boxes
   could be empty! A judge wrote:

   "It has never been held, so far as I am able to discover, that
   a bank has the right or is under an obligation to see that the
   description of the merchandise contained in the documents
   presented is correct." (August, p. 633)

   The Uniform Customs and Practices code of the international cham-
   ber of commerce states that "banks assume no liability for the form,
   sufficiency, accuracy, genuineness, falsification or legal effect of any
   documents." As a result, one of the usual documents is a certificate
   of inspection.
4. Prior to the issuance of the letter of credit, the seller may make
   sizeable investments (e.g. in designing the good, adding production
   capacity, or purchasing inputs) for which it may not be paid if the
   deal collapses. This is true of domestic transactions as well but
   again it is exacerbated for international transactions.

A large amount of trade avoids some of these informational problems
by avoiding "anonymous" relationships. One approach is to construct
business networks that transcend geography and national borders. Examples include Chinese ethnic trading networks, and multinational corporations. Another possibility is for outsiders to gain access to foreign
networks via "network intermediaries" such as the *Sogo Sosha* trading
houses of Japan. This might be compared to a house buyer who, upon
moving to an unfamiliar city, hires a real estate agent to help find the
desired type of property.

Appendix: INCO Terms

The abbreviations used in Figure 4.2 are defined and discussed in this appendix. It draws extensively on `www.jus.uio.no/lm//icc.incoterms.1990/doc.html`.

EXW (... named place): "Ex works" means that the seller fulfils his obligation to deliver when he has made the goods available at his premises (i.e. works, factory, warehouse, etc.) to the buyer...The buyer bears all costs and risks involved in taking the goods from the seller's premises to the desired destination.

FAS (... named port of shipment): "Free Alongside Ship" means that the seller fulfils his obligation to deliver when the goods have been placed alongside the vessel on the quay or in lighters at the named port of shipment. This means that the buyer has to bear all costs and risks of loss of or damage to the goods from that moment. The FAS term requires the buyer to clear the goods for export. It should not be used when the buyer cannot carry out directly or indirectly the export formalities. This term (and FOB) can only be used for sea or inland waterway transport.

FOB (... named port of shipment): "Free on Board" means that the seller fulfils his obligation to deliver when the goods have passed over the ship's rail at the named port of shipment. This means that the buyer has to bear all costs and risks of loss of or damage to the goods from that point.

CFR (... named port of destination): "Cost and Freight" Seller has responsibility to deliver the goods to the buyer's port and to turn over two documents: the invoice (cost) and the bill of lading (freight).

CIF (... named port of destination): "Cost, Insurance and Freight" means that the seller has the same obligations as under CFR but with the addition that he has to procure marine insurance against the buyer's risk of loss of or damage to the goods during the carriage. The seller contracts for insurance and pays the insurance premium. This term can only be used for sea and inland waterway transport. When the ship's rail serves no practical purposes such as in the case of roll-on/roll-off or container traffic, the CIP (Cost and Insurance Paid to...named place) term is more appropriate to use.

DEQ (... named port of destination): "Delivered Ex Quay (duty paid)" means that the seller fulfils his obligation to deliver when he has made the goods available to the buyer on the quay (pronounced "kee", it is a synonym of wharf) at the named port of destination, cleared for importation. The seller has to bear all risks and costs including duties, taxes and other charges of delivering the goods thereto (unless otherwise specified).

DDP (... named place of destination): "Delivered duty paid" means that the seller fulfils his obligation to deliver when the goods have been made available at the named place in the country of importation. The seller has to bear the risks and costs, including duties, taxes and other charges of delivering the goods thereto, cleared for importation. This term may be used irrespective of the mode of transport.

1. EXW is the sum of production costs and the markup.
2. FAS adds the cost of transporting the good from the manufacturer's premises to the port of export to the EXW price.
3. FOB adds the cost of loading the goods on board to the FAS price.
4. CIF adds the cost of shipping over water, including insurance of goods to the FOB price.
5. DEQ (duty paid) adds the cost of the duties to the CIF price.
6. DDP adds the cost of inland transport to the buyer's premises to the DEQ.

How should one choose which terms to use in quoting a price? One would be tempted to think the exporter should always want to quote EXW and leave all the risk and costs of export to the importer. Conversely the importer would prefer DDP, since it would be great to know the final price at the importer's premises. However, economic analysis suggests that burdens should be undertaken by whichever party can do so at lowest cost. Now it is likely that one or more third parties will actually be in charge of transporting the goods so it might not matter whether the exporter or importer is nominally responsible. In reality, however, the exporter usually will have an informational advantage (based on experience) in shipping within his country and the same will be true for the importer. Thus price quotes in CIF or FOB are reasonably common and EXW and DDP are fairly rare. Conventional practice seems to be that the importer is responsible for moving the good through customs in his home country. As a result, DEQ (duty paid) seems to be used rarely, if ever.

The Department of Commerce of the US recommends CIF:

When quoting a price, the exporter should make it meaningful to the prospective buyer. For example, a price for industrial machinery quoted "EXW Saginaw, Michigan, not export packed" is meaningless to most prospective foreign buyers. These buyers would find it difficult to determine the total cost and might hesitate to place an order.

The exporter should quote CIF or CIP whenever possible, as it shows the foreign buyer the cost of getting the product to or near the desired country.

An interesting option that some exporting firms have started to use is to form an alliance with a firm in the importing country that can handle costs such as duties and local freight charges. This allows the exporter to quote a DDP price which might be very attractive to a final buyer that is unfamiliar with the importing process.

References

The Economist, 2001, "Survey: European Business and the Euro" November 29th.

The Economist, 2002, "EU sauce policy," January 5th, p. 61.

Disdier, Anne-Celia and Keith Head, forthcoming, "The Puzzling Persistence of the Distance Effect on Bilateral Trade," *Review of Economics and Statistics*.

Hummels, David, 1999, "Towards a Geography of Trade Costs."

Hummels, David, 2000, "Time as a Trade Barrier."

International Business Training, "INCOTERMS 2000: Chart of Responsibility," ⟨www.i-b-t.net/incoterms.html⟩.

Neipert, David M., 2000, *A Tour of International Trade*, Prentice Hall.

5

Trade Rules

In 1931, the U.S. had average tariffs of 48% on manufactured imports. By the time the Uruguay Round of tariff reductions were phased in, its tariffs had fallen to an average of 3%. Similar reductions occurred in European nations, Japan, and Canada. An exception to the current general situation of low tariffs is the trade policy of countries that are not members of the World Trade Organization (WTO). For instance, prior to joining the WTO, China imposed high tariffs, import licensing, as well as numerous trade-related measures affecting foreign investors (content rules, exchange balancing, export requirements).

Finally, we will turn to additional trade liberalization measures.

5.1 National Trade Policies

It is useful to divide national trade policies into two categories. The first comprises the normal procedures and duties each would-be importer faces when attempting to clear customs. Then we turn to "special import measures" a term used by the Canadian government but which serves as a handy label for a diverse set of policies that are also referred to as "contingent protection."

5.1.1 Standard Customs Procedures

In the EU, US, Canada, and Japan basic tariffs on imports are low. For instance, Canada's 2002 MFN tariffs averaged 6.8% (down from 7.7% in 1998). MFN means "most-favoured nation." Normally, a member of the WTO is supposed to offer all members its MFN tariff. In practice there are many exceptions to this obligation. In Canada's case, the true most-favoured nation is the United States with whom Canada has had nearly tariff-free trade since January 1, 1998. However, total import duties were about 1% of total imports. This is because most Canadian trade occurs in products with zero duties.[1]

Even in the developing world, countries such as Mexico, Brazil, and Chile embarked on unilateral tariff reductions. Mexico and Brazil have continued to reduce tariffs in the regional agreements they joined in the early 1990s: NAFTA and Mercosur. Nevertheless, the low *average* level of tariffs hides substantial amounts of protection provided to textile products (fabrics, clothing, and shoes) and agricultural products in most high-income countries. Canada has average tariffs of 11.6% for footwear and 237% for dairy products.

The mere existence of customs duties imposes additional costs beyond the tariffs themselves. There are three things every importer must do before customs can be cleared.

1. *Classification*: The tariff schedule provides a duty for each tariff item (Canada has 8,364), identified with an 8-digit code. For statistical purposes there are two additional digits that must be added, leading to a 10-digit classification number. Examples are provided in Table 5.1.
2. *Valuation*: As most duties are assessed as a percent of the "customs value," the total amount to be paid depends on the value assigned to the shipment. Valuation involves starting with a transaction price and making certain adjustments.
3. *Origin-nation*: Provide documentation establishing the country of origin of the product and the "point of direct shipment." This is required to take advantage of preferential tariff rates.

Classification can sometimes involve rather arbitrary distinctions. For instance, *The Economist* reports (January 5th, 2002, p. 61 "EU Sauce Policy") that the European Union imposes a 20% duty on imported "sauces" and a 288% duty on imported vegetables. A firm exporting a can of vegetables to Europe thus has an incentive to call it a vegetable sauce. Wary of this, European regulations state that a sauce consisting of more than 20% "lumps" of vegetables is to be classified as a vegetable.

Before 1988 most countries had their own systems of classifying goods for customs duties. Then countries agreed upon a harmonized system of six-digit codes. The system is now employed by over 170 countries, representing about 98% of world trade. The harmonized sys-

---

[1] For details on average tariffs for a large number of countries, see the "Trade Policy Reviews" at ⟨www.wto.org⟩

Table 5.1. Extract from Canada's customs duty schedule

HS6	CCRA#	Description	MFN	GPT	LDCT+FTAs
95.06.11	1000	Downhill skis	0%	0%	0%
	9010	Cross-country skis	7.5%	5%	0%
	9020	Snowboards	7.5%	5%	0%
95.06.12	0000	Ski bindings	7%	5%	0%
95.06.19	0010	Ski poles	6.5%	3%	0%
95.06.21	0000	Sailboards	9.5%	6%	0%
95.06.29	0010	Water skis	7.5%	5%	0%
95.06.29	0090	Other (inc. surfboards)	7.5%	5%	0%
95.06.70	1100	Ice skates w/ boots	18%	18%	0%
95.06.70	2010	Ice skates w/o boots	5.5%	3%	0%
95.06.99	9089	Other (inc. skateboards)	7.5%	5%	0%

Note: HS6 are the 6-digit Harmonized System codes. CCRA# are the 4-digit Canada-specific codes. MFN is Most Favoured Nation status and it is offered to all WTO members and most other countries, with rare exceptions such as North Korea and Libya. GPT is General Preferential Tariff and it is offered to poorer countries including most of South America and Asia. LDCT is the Least Developed Countries tariff and it covers a smaller group of the world's poorest nations, including Haiti and most of Sub-Saharan Africa.

tem facilitates trade negotiations and makes international trade statistics easier to compare. Because individual countries want additional freedom to set tariffs and collect data based on particular national conditions, the full classification of a good starts with the HS6 and then adds four extra digits. The first two digits, combined with the HS6, form the 8-digit "tariff item." The last two digits do not affect duties but they are used for statistical purposes. For example, consider the case of snow skis, classified as 95.06.11 by all users of the HS. In Canada there are two tariff items, 10 and 90, receiving MFN rates of 0% and 7.5% respectively. For statistical purposes, Canada keeps track of 9010 (cross-country) and 9020 (snowboards) separately. In the US, on the other hand, the tariff items are 20 (cross-country skis, duty-free) and 40 (other, duty of 2.6%). One is left to speculate about why Canadians protect cross-country skis but Americans protect downhill skis.

Table 5.1 illustrates some potentially disputable issues. If you import bindings for a snowboard, would they be subject to 6.5% (ski bindings) or 7.5% (snowboards) tariffs? If you imported skis with built-in bindings would they be tariff-free? Eventually the Canada Customs and Revenue Agency (CCRA) would issue a ruling.

Establishing the origin of products being imported can be very simple or outrageously complex. For small shipments (less than \$1,600 in Canada) or for some basic levels of preferences (GPT or LDCT in Canada) it is sufficient to produce a "statement of origin" signed by the exporter (i.e. the firm the importer bought the product from). The firm might also need some supporting material to document that most of the production costs for the good were for inputs supplied in the exporting country.

> **EXPORTERS STATEMENT OF ORIGIN:**
> I certify that the goods described in this invoice or in the attached invoice # _____ were produced in the beneficiary country of _____ and that at least _____ per cent of the ex-factory price of the goods originates in the beneficiary country/countries of _____.

To claim tariff preferences within a free trade agreement can be much harder. For example suppose Sony wants to import a television from it's Mexico factory into the US or Canada. The MFN tariff rate is about 6% but the North American Free Trade Agreement (NAFTA) rate is zero. To qualify for the NAFTA rate, an importer will have to turn in a NAFTA certificate of origin that certifies that good meets NAFTA's detailed "rules of origin." These rules vary across products and it is very difficult to make generalizations about them. In most cases, the key to establishing origin lies in local sourcing of the most important components. In the case of televisions, the cathode ray tube (and a few other parts) must be made in North America.

Some importers employ the services of agents who specialize in moving goods through the customs procedures. The agents are called "custom brokers."[2] The costs of customs brokers vary but a former student, Lyle Herstein '00, reports "The percentage is rarely more than 1% of the shipment value up to something like a maximum charge of \$500.00."

5.1.2 Special Import Measures

Although standard tariffs have been lowered substantially, exporters still face important limits on free market access. The difference is that barriers today are more likely to be triggered by actions of the exporter than before when they were part of a nation's overall trade policy.

The most common form of Special Import Measures (SIMs) are punitive duties on "unfair" imports:

---

[2] "Freight-forwarders" are intermediaries who handle both logistics and customs.

1. Antidumping (AD) duties are triggered by pricing to an export market at less than the *normal* or "fair" value of the good.
2. Countervailing (CV) duties are triggered by government subsidies to the exporter.   补偿

Even if the exporter has not engaged in any "unfair" practices he may face safeguard protection in the following two forms:

1. "Escape Clause" safeguards that are permitted under GATT. These are temporary import restrictions (usually, but not necessarily, tariffs) designed to give the import-competing firms "breathing room" to adjust to a sudden surge in imports.
2. Voluntary Restraint Agreements (VRA). Also known as VERs (voluntary export restrictions) and OMAs (orderly marketing agreements), these are quotas on exports that are administered by the exporting nation's government. VRAs were considered a "grey area" prior to the Uruguay Round; that is, they were not prohibited but they were in violation of the spirit of GATT. Now new VRAs would probably be judged to be in violation of GATT if they were challenged.[3]

SIMs are administered by the importing country. Domestic firms competing with imports often exert substantial influence over the implementation of these policies. Not surprisingly, to protect their exporters' interests governments have sought to use the WTO to limit arbitrary usage of SIMs. In the next section we introduce the WTO and its rules restraining national trade policies. Then we will turn to consideration of the four main policies that the WTO attempts to constrain: antidumping duties, countervailing duties, safeguards, and disguised restrictions.

5.2 The World Trade Organization

The World Trade Organization (WTO) was established in 1994 as part of the Uruguay Round of the General Agreement on Tariffs and Trade. While the WTO's name gives the impression of immense powers, the WTO focuses on a more modest set of activities:

1. Organize talks for multilateral tariff cuts.
2. Establish rules to govern trading relationships.

---

[3] Canada's agreement to limit exports of softwood lumber to the US is a recent example of a VRA.

3. Resolve disputes over application of these rules.

The WTO and the General Agreement on Tariffs and Trade (GATT) that preceded it are essentially forums in which member countries agree to keep their import tariffs below certain levels called "bindings." Each member agrees to allow trade partners to export to their markets while paying moderate or no tariffs in exchange for the similar treatment in exporting to their markets. The members agree further that they will treat each other equally. Oddly enough, the principle that there should be no discriminatory treatment of WTO members is called the Most-Favoured Nation (MFN) principle.

Tariff bindings would have little value if countries simply substituted tariff barriers for a variety of other barriers such as quotas, import licenses, or discriminatory taxes and regulations. Hence countries also agree not to "nullify or impair" WTO member access to their markets.

Table 5.2. The main GATT rules and their exceptions

Members should	Except for
Treat all WTO members equally (MFN non-discrimination principle)	Free-Trade Areas, Custom Unions (Article XXIV)
Treat imported goods no worse than domestic "like products" (National Treatment principle)	Health Protection, Conservation (Article XX)
Use tariffs, not quotas (No quantitative restrictions)	"Safeguards" (Article XIX)
Set tariffs at/below "bindings"	Antidumping, Countervailing duties (Articles VI, XVI)

When one country feels that another WTO member is breaking the rules, the WTO serves as a dispute resolution forum as well. Disputes between members of the WTO are handled as follows:

"If one government believes that another is blocking its imports in breach of WTO rules, it can ask for talks. If these fail to resolve the dispute, the complaining government can ask for a panel of trade officials to adjudicate. If the panel finds the rules have been broken, the "guilty" party is supposed to amend its

laws or practice to conform with WTO rules. Appeals are possible, but once a final decision is reached, it can be blocked only by a consensus of WTO members. This is a big change from the old GATT system, under which every member (including guilty parties) had the right of veto. So far, no one has ignored a panel decision, because no one wants to jeopardize the credibility of the system of rule-based trade. But if someone did, the offended party could eventually retaliate with trade sanctions of its own."
Source: *The Economist* October 3, 1998, "Turtle wars."

5.3 Dumping

Definition: Dumping is the act of charging a price to the export market that is less than the normal value. The dumping *margin* is the percentage difference between normal value and the export price. Dumping is a form of *price discrimination*.

5.3.1 Developments in Antidumping Policy

Antidumping policy has a long history. The United States first addressed the issue in 1916. However, the original law required evidence of "predatory" intent. There were no successful cases under the 1916 law and the US introduced a new law in 1921 which set up the current system (used by most countries) under which there are two determinations: (1) if dumping has occurred, (2) if dumping has caused injury in the importing country. The original act of GATT in 1947 "condemns" dumping if "it causes or threatens material injury to an established industry in the territory of a Contracting Party or materially retards the establishment of a domestic industry."

When I wrote the first draft of this chapter, relying on data from the 1980s, only 12 countries (the EU is considered a single country for these purposes because it has a single commercial policy) were using antidumping laws. Furthermore, 95% of the cases were brought by the "Big 4": USA, EU, Canada, and Australia. In the 1995–2006 period there were 38 users and the not-so-big-4 accounted for less than a third of the measures imposed.

Between 1995 and June 2006 WTO members imposed 1875 new anti-dumping measures. The top 10 users and targets of anti-dumping measures are shown in Table 5.3.

Table 5.3. Who's dumping on whom? 1995–2006

User	number	share (%)	Target	number	share (%)
India	323	17.2	China	353	18.8
USA	236	12.6	EU	236	12.6
EU	224	11.9	Korea	132	7.0
Argentina	149	7.9	Taiwan	103	5.5
S. Africa	116	6.2	USA	100	5.3
Turkey	97	5.2	Japan	94	5.0
Canada	84	4.5	Russia	84	4.5
China, P.R.	83	4.4	Thailand	72	3.8
Mexico	82	4.4	Brazil	69	3.7
Australia	69	3.7	India	69	3.7

Given their size as importers, it is not surprising that the US and EU remain among the largest users of anti-dumping duties (ADDs). What shocked me in preparing this table was that India had vaulted to being the number one user. With the exception of the EU and US, the other targets tend not to be the biggest users. India and the US seem under-targeted relative to their usage, whereas East Asian exporters are over-targeted.

The total amount of trade directly affected by ADDs is fairly small. According the March 2006 Trade Policy Review conducted by the WTO, just 0.4% of all US imports between 1980 and 2003 were affected by anti-dumping measures. However, the policy indirectly affects a much larger share of trade by discouraging firms from pricing aggressively in foreign markets. Other countries have been learning how to "play the game" and we may expect to see even more countries pursuing aggressive AD policies in the future. On the other hand, two regional agreements (the EU and Australia-New Zealand) have eliminated antidumping duties between members. The NAFTA permits its members to target each other with anti-dumping duties. However, actions may now be appealed to NAFTA panels which have representation from the three members.

5.3.2 Antidumping Procedures in the US, EU, and Canada

Petitions for an antidumping investigation can come from a variety of complainants. "Eligible petitioners include manufacturers, producers, or wholesalers of a product that is like the investigated imports, or unions, other groups of workers, or certain other associations of such manufacturers, producers or wholesalers." (United States International

Trade Commission) The petitioners must jointly account for a significant part of domestic production (over 25%). Government agencies (such as the US Department of Commerce or the European Commission) may initiate investigations on their own.

After receiving a petition, a preliminary decision is made on both the issue of potential for injury and whether price is less than normal value. The standard of proof is quite low for potential injury. If the dumping margin is less than 2% or the petitioner is found not to represent the industry or to be unwilling to provide reasonable amounts of information, then the case will be thrown out. Final determinations of dumping and injury may take several months.

The dumping determination

Let us define P_x as the export price. More precisely it is the price charged for exports prior to paying for transport costs of reaching the market or any duties. Thus, P_x is the FOB price. Let P_n be the "normal value" of the good. The first definition of P_n is simply the price the exporter charges to domestic consumers (naturally, it should also be a "factory door" price which does not include transport costs or taxes.)

Suppose the exporting firm does not sell the good in his home market (e.g. golf carts from Poland). Then P_n may be set equal to the price charged for exports to a third market.

Suppose there is a domestic price but it is deemed unsuitable. Why? Perhaps because the exporter's home country is not a market economy so there are no true market-determined prices. Alternatively, suppose the price the exporter charges to domestic consumers is below average cost. This also is deemed "unfair." As a result, in determining the normal price, all sales at prices below average cost are excluded.

If there is not sufficient information to obtain a normal price (perhaps because of pervasive pricing below average cost) then one is constructed as the sum of production costs plus overhead plus a "reasonable" profit margin. In the EU and Canada an attempt is made to calculate the actual average profit margin on profitable sales. In the EU, that has resulted in considerable variability (5% to 60%). Canada will use 8% as the profit margin if it cannot obtain reliable measures. The US does not use actual data on overhead or profit margins and simply uses 10% for the former and 8% for the latter.

In the US (and probably the other users of ADDs) it seems to be fairly easy to show dumping. About 95% of all cases end up with positive dumping findings. However, it is harder to prove injury.

The injury determination

Injury has a very broad definition. Most countries' rules instruct the agency determining injury to look at the complaining industry's output, employment, capacity utilization, profits, investment, and inventories. In particular, attention seems to be paid to whether import shares rose during the dumping period (the agency may look at several years of data) and whether prices were forced down by the dumped imports.

One key element of the injury determination is defining the domestic industry. Usually the petitioners will try to set the definition so that any domestic firms who are prospering will be counted as producing a different product. In the US firms cannot be counted as part of the domestic industry if they are "related"; that is, if they have close ties to the exporter or the importing agent. In the US the amount of imports considered to be potentially causing injury is obtained by summing up all the imports of countries that were found to have dumped. Note that this gives an incentive to bring dumping cases against as many foreign nations as possible so that it will be easier to establish injury. In determining injury, the agencies are instructed to consider other potential causes of poor performance by domestic firms, e.g., a slump in overall demand or poor management.

The magnitude and duration of ADDs

The duty is set equal to the dumping margin. It is designed to exactly offset the impact of dumping, thereby restoring price to the "normal" or "fair" value.

In the US, as soon as the preliminary duty is determined, "liquidation" is suspended and the duty is owed. The firm importing the good will have to post a bond or make a deposit to cover the cost of the duty. The actual amount owed will only be known when the final dumping margin is determined, which could be 135 days later. The importer is liable for the dumping margin on all imports.

In Europe and Canada, the duties are not applied until after the final duty is determined. In Canada at that time, a "normal" value is set and no duty is owed if the export price exceeds normal value. It seems that the EU can charge retroactively for up to 90 days prior to the determination of the dumping duty.

In principle, the duties should end when the dumping ends. In practice, it appears that the duties may continue for indefinite periods. The Uruguay Round compelled countries who use AD laws to review each case after 5 years to see if there is still injury. This is called the "sunset" provision.

5.3.3 Strategies for Coping with Antidumping

What options does the exporting firm face when it is facing an antidumping case?

Exit If the market is not too large and prospects are limited, the firm might opt to just stop exporting and abandon the market. This is not likely to be an attractive option if the country imposing the ADD is the US or EU or any other significant market.

Settle One option the foreign firm has is to agree immediately to charge higher prices, and/or limit exports. This may be an excellent opportunity for a group of exporters to form a cartel and charge high prices. About a third of US antidumping cases are dropped, mostly because of "undertakings" to raise the price.

Litigate It may be difficult to show injury. Depending on how fair the members of the commission are, chances of winning may not be terrible. About a third of US AD cases result in a finding of no injury. Even if the firm ultimately loses, it can then raise the price. Under the US system, a firm may request "administrative review" in which it attempts to show that it has stopped dumping and therefore should have some duties reimbursed.

Circumvent Engage in foreign direct investment as an alternative to exporting. The firm could simply open up a final assembly plant in the target market and import the parts. Alternatively, assembly could be done in a third country. The US and EU have adopted anticircumvention policies to try to stop this. To be on safe ground, the firm would want to set up the plant in advance and carry out a fairly large amount of value-added in the host country.

5.4 Subsidies and Countervailing Duties

The WTO "Agreement on Subsidies and Countervailing Measures" attempts to do two things. First, it describes certain actions that member governments are not allowed to do. Second, it regulates how they can respond to subsidies offered by other governments.

The Basic Definition: Subsidies are financial contributions by a government or any public body that confer a benefit.

Financial contributions may include loans, loan guarantees, certain tax credits, government provision of goods or services other than basic infrastructure. The WTO rules only apply to subsidies that are *specific*. The idea is a subsidy available to all firms and all industries is not distortionary. However, a subsidy offered to a set of enterprises based on their industry or region would be considered specific. The WTO also distinguishes between two types of subsidies.

Prohibited subsidies are those that are contingent in law or in fact on exporting or on using domestic rather than imported inputs (local content).

Actionable subsidies are allowed by the WTO but countries that can show that they are hurt by such subsidies are allowed to respond to them with countervailing duties. Thus, if a subsidy is based on total production without regard to whether the output is exported, it would be allowable. However, if some member of the WTO can show that its firms were injured by subsidized imports either at home or in a third market, then those members can apply countervailing duties.

There are exceptions to the subsidies rules for agricultural products and for very poor countries.

5.5 Safeguards

Article 19 of GATT allows members to impose import restrictions if a surge in imports causes injury to a domestic industry. Although this allows for protection without having to prove the existence of an "unfair" trade practice such as dumping or subsidies, it has not been used very frequently. The potential reasons for lack of use are as follows:

1. The Most-Favoured-Nation clause of GATT would seem to require the importing country to impose the trade barrier on all sources of imports. Usually, as in the motorcycle case of 1984, the importing country just wants to restrict imports of a particular competitor.
2. GATT requires the importing country to compensate the exporting countries by lowering trade barriers in other industries. If satisfactory compensation is not provided the exporting countries may use retaliatory tariffs.
3. Protection must be temporary: In the US, tariffs had to be phased out over 5 years.
4. In the US, safeguards require presidential authorization which is something the President may not be willing to give or the industry may be reluctant to ask for (Reagan authorized protection in 11 out of 32 cases that reached him).

These considerations help explain why ADDs and negotiated quantitative restrictions (which GATT-speak refers to as Voluntary Restraint Agreements or VRAs) were much more popular with the domestic industries and the government entities that wished to protect them from imports. Recall that dumping is usually easy to establish and if there are positive dumping and injury findings, a duty is imposed automatically in the US.[4] VRAs are politically attractive for negotiators because they give higher prices to the foreign exporters which may make their home governments less likely to complain to the WTO or retaliate (on the other hand they do not generate tariff revenues but this may not concern the pro-industry negotiators).

5.6 Disguised Protection

National Treatment requires that once goods have entered a market (i.e. after applicable duties have been paid), they must be treated no less favourably than domestically-produced goods. This means that governments are not supposed to adopt regulations or set taxes in such a way as to "afford protection" to the domestic industry. The reasoning here is simple. A country could make itself appear to have free trade by eliminating all of its customs duties while replacing them with a mix of regulations and taxes that had the same impact on imports. For example, suppose France eliminates a 10% tariff on imported cheese but then puts a 10% tax on all cheese made from animals that do not reside in France. This tax has the same effect on consumer prices as the tariff. The difference comes only from the way the money is collected.

The difficulty with applying the national treatment principle is that the original GATT agreement made some explicit exceptions.

An example might be that the Japanese government has a list of approved ingredients for cosmetics and that list corresponds to the ingredients used by Japanese manufacturers but not foreign manufacturers. The Japanese could invoke the human-animal-plant health exception from National Treatment. They have apparently argued that Japanese skin is different from foreign skin and hence requires these protections. Under the Uruguay Round, however, governments must establish that health and safety restrictions are based on *scientific* principles. It is possible that the different skin argument would not be considered scientifically sound.

---

[4] In Canada, there is still the possibility that the duty will be considered against national interest and hence not imposed.

Following are some notable cases where a home country imposed regulations or banned import and foreign exporters complained to the World Trade Organization that these practices constituted a form of disguised protection.

US Embargo of Mexican Tuna The US banned imports of tuna caught using technologies that kill significant numbers of dolphins. The GATT panel considered this a quantitative restriction. Although countries are allowed to impose quantitative restrictions for the safety of their own environment, GATT ruled that the way tuna is caught does not affect the tuna consumed in the US and hence could not affect the American environment.

US Gasoline Standards The Clean Air Act mandated that gasoline sold in certain highly polluted cities be "reformulated" to lower pollution. Simultaneously it forbid refiners from "degrading" the "conventional" gasoline that they sold for use in the other cities. That is a standard was imposed not on the *level* of quality of conventional gasoline but on *changes* in that quality. Domestic refiners were given the option of maintaining the individual baseline they currently used in refining (as of 1990) or adhering to the "statutory" baseline. Foreign refiners did not have this option; they had to adhere to the statutory baseline. Refiners from Brazil and Venezuela claimed this was a disguised restriction and hence a violation of the GATT principle of national treatment. The US argued that it was not feasible to verify and enforce individual baselines for foreign refiners. A WTO panel found in favour of Brazil and Venezuela. It said the US could either impose a statutory baseline for domestic and imported refiners or allow individual baselines for both in all cases where it was verifiable and enforceable and only use the statutory baseline where this was not the case.

Japanese Liquor This case (ruled on by a WTO panel on July 11, 1996) involves taxation policy. In Japan liquor made from potatoes, buckwheat and other grains, known as *shochu* is taxed at roughly $3.50 per litre whereas other liquors pay much higher taxes, as high as $23.00 per litre for Scotch whiskey (defined by www.dictionary.com as "an alcoholic liquor distilled from grain, such as corn, rye, or barley, and containing approximately 40 to 50 percent ethyl alcohol by volume.") Imports make up just 8% of Japan's liquor consumption, compared to 30% for Germany and 35% for the US. Using 1994 data, the average unit value of liquor exported to Japan was about $6 per litre. Thus, we might see these high taxes on whiskey as equivalent to more than 100% import tariffs. The Japanese maintained that whiskey and other liquors typically produced abroad were not "like products" to *shochu* and hence they need not have the same taxes. (*Shochu* is a clear liquid usually diluted with warm water before drinking.) They pointed out that Japanese-made whiskey pays the same tax as foreign whiskey. The WTO was not persuaded and found against the Japanese, ordering them to make changes in the tax policy. Part of the panel's argument was that the current separation of whiskey and shochu as "low" and "high" end products is not exogenous, but rather the consequence of the tax differences that make whiskey unaffordable for Japanese workers. The claim is that they would be viewed as close substitutes if they were subjected to similar tax rates.

"Split-run" Magazines in Canada: Some US magazines sell Canadian editions which are mainly the same as the US edition but contain a small number of Canada-oriented articles. They would like to sell advertising space in the Canadian editions to Canadian companies that wish to advertise to Canadian readers. This has been vehemently opposed by the Canadian magazine industry which argues that it cannot compete with split-run editions in the market for selling advertising space. Under the justification of protecting Canadian culture, the Canadian government has repeatedly attempted to prevent split-run magazines from carrying Canadian advertising. Three policies have been used. First there was a ban at the border which Sports Illustrated circumvented by beaming its editorial content into Canada via satellite. Next, Canada instituted an 80% tax on advertising revenues of split-run editions of foreign magazines. It also created a postal subsidy for Canadian magazines. All three measures were ruled to be in violation of Canada's trade obligations by a WTO panel in 1997. In 1999, Canada was still attempting to block split-run magazines selling of advertising space in Canada. Meanwhile the US threatened retaliation against a large range of Canadian products. Eventually a deal would be negotiated.

5.7 Preferential Trade Agreements

A trade agreement is "preferential" when it gives the member countries better access to each others' markets than non-members. Article I of GATT, the Most-Favoured-Nation (MFN) obligation, calls for each GATT member to grant to every other member the most favourable treatment which it grants to any country with respect to imports and exports of products. The purpose of the act was to replace the complex web of highly discriminatory bilateral agreements with a multilateral rules framework. However, Article XXIV of GATT makes an exception for two types of preferential trade agreements (PTAs): free-trade areas (FTAs) and customs unions.[5] When two countries form an FTA then they agree to eliminate most (or all) tariffs on each other's products. On goods from the rest of the world, they continue to charge the same tariffs as before, i.e. mainly their MFN tariffs—which could be very different from each other. For example, among the NAFTA members the US has the lowest average MFN tariff, 4.9% (2006 *Trade Policy Review*), then Canada at 6.8% (2003 *TPR*), followed by Mexico at 16.5% (2002 *TPR*). In contrast the members of a Customs Union give up the ability to choose their own tariffs and charge a *common external tariff*.

For an agreement to be GATT-compliant, the following two conditions must be met.

1. The countries forming the agreement liberalize "substantially all" the trade between them.
2. The group is not "on the whole" more restrictive towards outsiders than they were before.

Some FTAs have dubious records in actually eliminating "substantially all" of their former "duties and other restrictive regulations of commerce." One reason is that the same exceptions that GATT allows its members (anti-dumping, health and safety) are also allowed for PTA members. The second requirement is usually easy for FTAs to meet since their MFN tariffs are already bound by prior GATT negotiations. It is trickier for customs unions. Unless they choose the lowest of their members' prior tariffs, at least some members will have higher tariffs after joining. If the customs union imposes higher average tariffs than the original members had, then they are expected to compensate other GATT members for the loss in market access.

5.7.1 The European Union

The European Union (formerly the European Economic Community) was founded in 1958. Membership has grown steadily, adding Greece, Portugal, and Spain in the 1980s and Sweden, Austria, and Finland in 1995. The 2004 accession of 10 mainly Eastern European nations saw the EU taking on more members than in any prior expansion.

---

[5] The WTO website refers to PTAs as RTAs where the R stands for Regional. The reason why many economists resist this abbreviation is that a significant number of current PTAs can not reasonably be called regional, e.g. Canada's FTA with Israel.

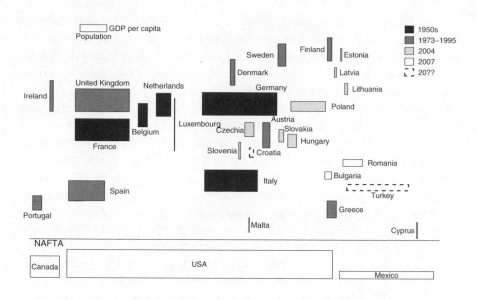

Fig. 5.1. An "economic map" of the EU and NAFTA

Considered as a single entity, the EU has the world's highest GDP (over US$13 trillion) and is Canada's second largest trade partner.

Figure 5.1 displays the 25 member states of the EU shaded according to when they joined. The width of each country rectangle shows it's population and the heights show income per capita. This means that areas depict GDPs. For comparison purposes, the three NAFTA members are shown at the base of the figure. One thing worth noting is that the most recent expansion incorporated countries that were often considerably poorer (flatter rectangles in the figure) than the original members. This has created economic tension because the EU not only facilitates trade between members, it also facilitates labour movement. At the time of writing, the likelihood of Turkey being allowed to join this decade seems low.

Trade between European Union members has been essentially free of tariffs and quotas since 1968. Nevertheless, 17 years later the European Commission argued that Europe's internal market was far from unified. The Commission issued a White Paper in 1985 that identified three primary barriers to intra-EU trade: differences in technical standards, delays and administrative burdens caused by frontier controls, and national biases in government procurement. The Commission then launched a research project to establish the costs of what they referred to as "Non-Europe" or the "present market fragmentation of the European Community" (Commission of the EC, 1988). By the time the 16-volume study was released, the member nations had already legislated the Single European Act (SEA). The Act contained roughly 300 proposals from the White Paper designed to "complete" Europe's internal market by the end of 1992.

There were three key elements of the 1987 Single European Act. The first was the attempt to reduce the cost imposed by crossing the border. A subset of the EU membership (Britain, Ireland, and Denmark did not participate) eliminated *frontier controls*. They also allowed *cabotage*. Thus, a trucking company based in France could now deliver freight from one German city to another. Even more ambitiously, the EU also began to harmonize technical standards. Finally, SEA aimed to reduce national-bias in government procurement by using transparent and open bidding processes to allocate government service contracts.

The final step towards economic integration taken by the European Union was the creation of a common currency. The Euro was phased in from 1999–2002 in twelve countries, sometimes called Euro-land. Two EU members, the UK and Denmark, are not legally required to join. The other members are supposed to join over the next few years. Some have plans to do so while others, notably Sweden, show little inclination.

5.7.2 The North American Free Trade Agreement

NAFTA took effect in January 1994. Immediately, two thirds of Mexican exports began to enter the US duty free (up from 14%) and almost half of US exports entered Mexico duty free (up from 18%). By 2009 all duties between Canada, US and Mexico will be eliminated. New NAFTA panels with representatives from all three were put in place to facilitate dispute resolution. They listen to appeals on antidumping and countervailing duty cases. Under Chapter 11 of NAFTA, there is also a provision for foreign firms to bring cases of alleged expropriation by the host government.

NAFTA may not have very large effects. At the time it took effect, Canada and the US were already in the sixth year of their FTA, so most duties were already eliminated between them. Even Mexico, thanks to a program of trade liberalization introduced in 1986, had substantially lowered its average tariffs. Also, Mexico is a small economy relative to the United States and its trade with Canada, while growing, remains fairly low. Furthermore, there are many less visible barriers that remain. In particular, there are significant hassles at the border. Corrupt practices have been reported and border delays are common. The major value of NAFTA might be as a way for US and Mexican governments to commit to free trade for the future against potential demands for protection.

References

Brander, James, 1995, *Government Policy Toward Business* Chapter 9, Wiley.

Croome, John, 1995, *Reshaping the World Trading System*, World Trade Organization.

General Accounting Office, 1994, *General Agreement on Tariffs and Trade: Uruguay Round Final Act Should Produce Overall U.S. Gains.* US Government Publishing Office.

Jackson, John, 1989, *The World Trading System* MIT Press.

Trebilcock, Michael and Robert Howse, 1995, *The Regulation of International Trade*, Routledge.

The World Trade Organization, *Trade Policy Review: Canada 2003* (Bernan: Lanham, MD).

The World Trade Organization, "International Trade Trends and Statistics."

International Monetary Fund, 1998, *Staff Country Report: Canada* No. 98/55, Chapter VIII. Developments in Canadian Trade Policy.

6

Market Adaptation

"A lotta the same [stuff] we got here, they got there, but there they're a little different." (Vincent Vega in *Pulp Fiction*).

In this chapter we consider the issue of positioning in what is called "product attribute space." This is the key question of the field of international marketing. Should a firm offer the same product worldwide or customize the product to suit the demands of each market? We refer to this as the standardization vs. adaptation issue.

The firm must decide whether to modify its product to better suit local buyer characteristics. Modifications may be limited to the way the product is promoted, i.e. the "message" sent out to consumers in an attempt to influence their *perceptions* of the product. In most cases the firm will need to consider modifying the objective attributes of the product. In some cases, the nature of the product attributes change so much that it effectively introduces a new product.

6.1 The Levitt Argument

In 1983 Theodore Levitt, a marketing professor at Harvard Business School, wrote an article that popularized the term "globalization" and called into question the received wisdom on international marketing strategy. Levitt advocated a move towards a "global corporation" that "sells the same things in the same way everywhere." In other words, corporations should sell standardized consumer products worldwide. Levitt's argument seems to boil down to three ideas.

Cosmopolitanism Advances in technology have increased cross-cultural communication. Primarily through the media of television and movies (the Internet in its current form did not exist at the time of Levitt's article), consumers everywhere have become aware of what their counterparts are buying. According to Levitt, American products have considerable allure—once seen, they appear irresistible. Levitt concluded "The world's needs and desires have become irrevocably homogenized."

Price Consumers will be drawn to low-priced high quality products even if they differ from the varieties that they traditionally consumed. By standardizing, the firm can lower unit costs and offer a more attractive price. "Manufacturers with minimal customization and narrow product-line breadth will have costs far below those with more customization and wider lines."

Promotion When surveyed, consumers in different nations will express preferences for particular product features. Firms must recognize that these stated preferences mainly reflect what the consumer is accustomed to buying. It is necessary to look behind such superficial preferences to the underlying needs and desires of the customer. These are likely to vary much less across countries. Advertising can be used to explain to customers how a different product actually satisfies their fundamental needs. Levitt's example is washing machines. Different Europeans claimed to prefer different spin speeds, capacities, and washing actions (tumble versus agitator). However, Levitt claimed, what they really wanted was an effective low-cost machine. When offered that option, their actual purchasing decisions often contradicted their expressed preferences.

Each of Levitt's points has some merit. Imitation does indeed seem to be a powerful force. In a world where we are more aware of the customs of foreigners we are more likely to copy them. Moreover it does seem like American popular culture is particularly "contagious." Nevertheless, imitation remains a force with a strong local bias. You are much more likely to imitate your neighbors and classmates than people living thousands of miles away. The experience of Tyco Toys in Europe provides an interesting illustration.[1]

For Mr. Austin [director of Tyco's European operations], the final straw came in October 1992, when he and Mr. Grey (CEO of Tyco) clashed over whether Matchbox should produce action figures and toy vehicles in Britain tied to a planned sequel for "Thunderbirds," a popular children's science-fiction TV show.

---

[1] "Too Much, Too Fast," *The Wall Street Journal* September 26, 1996 p. R8

At the time, Thunderbird items were Matchbox's most profitable European brand.

"The line Dick Grey gave to me was, 'We aren't going to do local development'" because Tyco preferred to promote global brands, Mr. Austin recollects. "I said, 'What if a local development makes money?' He said, 'Read my lips.'"

Mr. Austin abruptly quit, formed a toy business—and reaped $12 million in sales and $4 million in profit peddling the Thunderbird sequel's product line the following year.

Second, price is only one attribute. The willingness of consumers to substitute away from their ideal product and the cost savings from standardization both depend on quantitative estimates of response elasticities. Levitt presents no convincing evidence of large elasticities in either case. Finally, the expressed preferences of consumers should perhaps be taken a bit more seriously than Levitt suggests. A French consumer's stated preference for a front-loading, agitating washing machine might derive from his dryer fitting on top of his washer and his belief that the tumble action is too damaging to the thinner fabric in French clothing. It is quite possible that no amount of advertising would convince him to buy a top-loading tumble action washer.

Levitt's argument is helpful because it challenges the dogma that firms should always adapt to local market demands. However, there are clearly cases where demand differences do warrant product adaptations. We should conduct a case-by-case analysis of the costs and benefits of adaptation. Before turning to the details of such an analysis, we will first consider some actual examples.

6.2 Examples of Adaptation

As a way of familiarizing ourselves with the international marketing strategies that are actually used, we can go through the exercise of fitting examples into the following adaptation matrix.

"The Big Mac is the Big Mac, only in France, it's *Le Big Mac*." This quote from the film Pulp Fiction and the use of the Big Mac by *The Economist* to determine the relative price of a common good illustrate the idea that the Big Mac is virtually the same product everywhere it is sold.

Marcus James wines were a big success in the United States in the early1990s when their sales rose rapidly to become the number two

Table 6.1. The international marketing matrix

		"Message"	
		Standard	Adapted
Product	**Standard**	Coke, Big Mac, Marlboro	Marcus James Wines Green Giant, Cheer
	Adapted	Fax Machines, Pampers Nestle infant cereals	Ford Mr. Big

ranked imported wine. Although the wines are made by the Cooperativa Vinicola Aurora of Brazil, the label is designed to make them appear American. Initially, they did not even specify the country of origin.

Green Giant discovered that its canned sweet corn was consumed in very different ways in different countries (in salads in France, sandwiches in Britain, on ice cream in Korea, etc) and tailored the advertising message accordingly.

Nestle infant cereals vary across countries to make use of local raw materials (wheat in Europe, maize in Latin America, soya in Asia). This might be cost-driven rather than demand-driven adaptation.

Pampers in Japan are not the thick, more absorbent type sold in large packs that are found in the US. As Japanese mothers change diapers more frequently and have little storage space, Proctor and Gamble sells thinner diapers in smaller packages.

Cheer changed its advertising strategy for washing detergent in Japan once it realized that there is little value to being "All-temperature" if all the consumers wash with cold water only.

Ford hoped it might make the same car for sale around the world. In the end, it kept the same design and basic components but adapted the body and name to local markets. In the US it is referred to as the Contour (or Mystique when sold under the Mercury label) but elsewhere it is called the Mondeo. The North American versions is slightly "longer and sleeker" and it has a bigger trunk than the European version.

Mr. Big: Upon entering the Taiwanese market, Neilson's "Mr. Big" chocolate bar was marketed under the name of Bang Bang, which was a pre-existing local brand thought to have a good reputation. Upon entering Mexico, the Mr. Big name was preserved but the chocolate bar itself was "down-sized" to 40 grams (from a range of 43–65 in the US and Canada). In Mexico, Mr. Big is marketed under the distributor-owned label of "Milch," a word thought to connote "goodness and health."

Sometimes a company does not adapt the product or message it currently employs at home but rather draws upon its core competence in product design to create a new product, geared to be successful in the foreign market. Examples include the Mazda Miata (roadster designed for the US market), Ben & Jerry's Cool Brittania flavour of ice cream, Campbell's Duck Gizzard soup (for the Guangdong market), and Coca Cola's "Georgia" (a canned coffee developed for the Japanese market).

Along with McDonalds and Malboros, Coca Cola has come to be seen as an example of product that is essentially the same everywhere. I have to add "essentially" because I am told there are small differences in the formula used for different countries. The common aspects of Coke's taste and image are much more important than the subtle differences. Nevertheless, Coca Cola has recently reconsidered its stance of offering essentially one product to all markets (*New York Times* February 6, 2000). They plan to offer more locally popular beverages. One example where this has already been working is Japan. Brand Coke is only the third most popular product of the Coca Cola corporation in Japan, lagging behind canned coffees and teas. Nevertheless, while Japan represents only 5 percent of Coke's overall sales, it contributes 20 percent of company profits. In the long run it is not clear whether this success can be replicated elsewhere. In many cases indigenous companies will have a strong advantage in offering local drinks and Coke would have to work hard to gain credibility. Nonetheless, it is interesting to see that even one of the most famous "World" brands ever is not betting on all cultural differences in demands to disappear.

Why would a firm customize its product and/or message? The simplistic answer is to achieve a better fit to the market demands in each country. Why do market demands differ across countries?

One reason is that government regulations may require certain product specifications. This is usually done for health and safety concerns or to conform to local standards. Thus, the government regulatory differences are the outcome of other differences in the voters and consumers themselves. We will focus on the sources of the basic differences in demands and keep in mind that sometimes the government forces any firm that wishes to sell in a market to adapt to the local rules. In other cases, it may be the "market" itself that compels adaptation.

Recall from basic microeconomics that market demand curves are the sum of individual demand curves. The latter are the outcome of a consumer attempting to achieve the highest level of satisfaction given his preferences and the constraint that expenditures cannot exceed income. Consumers usually do not have preferences for specific products but rather for *attributes* of products. The set of desired attributes depends on both the characteristics of the buyer and the environment in which he resides.

This summary of demand curve determination suggests a number of sources of different demand curves in different countries. Following the six forms of separation, we can group the main sources of market demand differences into the following categories: environmental adaptations, developmental adaptations, and social adaptations.

6.3 Environmental Adaptations

Sometimes consumer behaviour differs across countries not because of fundamental differences in the people but rather in the environment in which they live. Thus, we see different "demands" that are actually responses to different sets of environmentally determined desires for attributes that solve particular problems. Adaptations of the products are required to make them suitable to the national environment.

- *Topography:* The presence of coastline, mountains, and other geographic features will influence demand. For example, trucks in mountainous countries need stronger axles and transmissions. High altitudes can require different cooking instructions.
- *Climate:* In wet climates, there will be greater demand for water-proofed shoes. In snowy climates, cars equipped with all-weather tires will be demanded. In very cold climates (like Alberta), cars need to be equipped with electric plugs so that they can be started in the morning.
- *Population Density:* Japanese and European cities differ from North American ones in that they are much more densely populated. This density makes space expensive which has a wide set of implications for product design. For example, cars need to be smaller to get around narrow streets and park in tight spots (In Houston, one need never learn how to parallel park). Dish-washing machines in France often have a stove on top. Refrigerators and pantries tend to

be smaller when land is scarce and this causes consumers to make more frequent food purchases.

- *Scarcity of complementary products:* The demand for certain attributes depends on the availability and cost of complementary goods and services. One example is that the demand for cars or air conditioners to be energy-efficient depends in large part on the price of gas and electricity. The demand for cell-phones to have internet features is thought to be higher in Europe where consumers tend to face a higher price for computer access to the internet.

6.4 Developmental Adaptations

Differences in economic development generate differences in the products demanded through several different mechanisms. The most important cause is the *Income effect.* There is a systematic relationship between high incomes and the demand for "luxuries" (high quality products, other non-necessities), from *lattes* to luxury cars. These relationships are called "Engel" curves. Furthermore, it appears that high income consumers tend to place a higher premium on product safety and health. There is a simple economic explanation for why this might be true: Extending one's life and lowering the probability of accidental death are more valuable to people who have high standards of living and therefore have more to gain from staying alive!

The sources of high average incomes that we uncovered in Chapter 1 also have direct influences on demands.

There are important *education effects.* Literacy and informedness influence demand (e.g. for computers or Internet services or health-related products). *Female participation* also affects demand. Men and women appear to have differences in the type of products they demand and also in their receptiveness to different promotional campaigns. The more women participate in the economy and in politics, the more strongly they will instate their preferences in aggregate demand.

6.5 Cultural Adaptation

Consumers from countries with similar natural environments and similar levels of economic development can still manifest very different demands for products. Furthermore, they are often receptive to different modes of communication. Cultural adaptation is a broad category that encompasses familiar aspects of culture such as religion and language. I will also use the term to refer to technical differences, such as voltage standards or measurement systems.

6.5.1 Traditions and Imprinting

To a large extent the past seems to govern people's current demands. We shall define "traditions" as the set of practices that individuals in a culture "inherit" from their elders, particularly their parents. Traditions represent the reliance of subsequent generations on solutions to problems that were discovered by early generations. As a result, the followers of tradition can benefit from the information gathered by the leaders without having to replicate their search costs. Examples include traditional recipes and remedies. Note that sometimes the external environment changes and traditional practices become mal-adapted for solving current problems. This would appear to be a situation in which advertising might be quite effective at causing change.

Imprinting is the process by which an individual's past experience causes their preferences to become inflexible. At the most basic level it may simply be that people from different countries have basic differences in the features of products that they find appealing. For instance, citizens of one country may like sweeter colas and chocolate than citizens of another country. The most likely explanation is imprinting. People tend to like things the way they grew up with them. They assume that what is familiar is right and natural. Foreign things, on the other hand, taste "strange."

6.5.2 Conformism and the Social Interaction Effect

For many types of behaviour, there is a form of *network externality*: The more individuals share a given practice, the more attractive (or less repulsive) that practice becomes to others. Table 6.2 presents a very simple framework in which we can be specific about social interaction effects. Consider the choice being "left" versus "right." This might be something practical such as the side of the road to drive on or it might be which political party one joins.

The amounts shown in the table are "My" payoffs. The variable I represents the individual's own basic preference for Left. In a political setting, one's childhood experiences may have led to certain conclusions about liberty, equality and other values that dictate political affiliation. The bigger I is, the more left-leaning the person's political inclinations.

Table 6.2. Social versus individual effects

		Majority Choice	
		Left	Right
	Left	$G + I$	I
My Choice			
	Right	0	G

A negative value of I means the individual prefers the Right. Right-handed people usually prefer to drive on the right side of the road, for instance, because left-hand steering arrangements let them use their right hand for gear shifting. In contrast, G represents the gain from conforming to behavior of the majority of the group. When $|G| > |I|$, social effects overwhelm individual preferences and it is in my own interest to conform with the group even if the majority decision differs from my own "individual" preference. Why might G be important? In the driving case, the obvious advantage of following the majority practice is to avoid head-on collisions! In the case of politics, most people have experienced the discomfort of expressing a minority viewpoint and being criticized as unfeeling or unthinking or both! Conformity, on the other hand, leads to reassurances that one's (expressed) views are indeed justified.

The situation where social effects are overpowering gives rise to two possible equilibria: Everyone might choose Left or everyone might choose Right. It is possible that a group might select Right even if all the individual members happened to prefer Left.[2] Thus it is not always a good idea to assume that just because a group behaves in a certain way that it reflects the actual values of the individual members. Rather, it might simply reflect the interplay of chance historical events and strong social interaction effects (SIEs).

Organized religions are influenced by both history (tradition) and conformism (social interaction effects). While we can certainly think of many examples of people who have turned away from the religion of their parents, the evidence suggests a strong tendency of children to

---

[2] This would not happen if people chose sequentially under full information. However, it could occur if historically I tended to be negative but it gradually changed over time. Then people might be "stuck" with "Right" if they cannot find a way to collectively switch to "Left."

follow their mothers' choice of religion. Group interaction effects also affect the practice of religion. In general it is much easier to observe the rules of a religion if one lives near other adherents. And, conversely, the social pressure on an individual to convert to the majority religion can be extremely powerful. Although religions are primarily oriented towards spiritual concerns, they also tend to involve a number of prescriptions and prohibitions that affect day-to-day life and therefore consumer demands. For instance, bans on alcohol are fairly common (Muslims and several Christian denominations). Some food types may be prohibited (beef by Hindus, pork by Jews and Muslims). There are sometimes rules on clothing as well (the Burka used in Afghanistan is a prominent recent example).

6.5.3 Communication Standards

Symbols are words, images, and gestures that convey a meaning to the observer. Most words in our language are symbols in that the sound has no relation to the meaning. For example, the important thing is that all English speakers know that "go" means to proceed whereas "stop" means to cease an action. In Spanish, "va" means go. The Chevrolet "Nova" became the target of derision in Spain because "no va" means "doesn't go." Even colours have symbolic consequences. In Anglo-Saxon cultures, yellow usually is associated with cowardice, whereas in China, it is a colour for royalty.

If a buyer and seller do not share common symbols, then they may not be able to communicate in a timely and effective manner and exchanges may be foregone. Sharing a common first language seems like it should matter less today now that English has become the normal language for most international business. However, statistical studies of trade find that country-pairs that share a common official language trade two to three times as much as pairs that speak different languages.

One particular type of symbol that is of great importance is what economists refer to as *signals*. These are forms of behaviour that individuals use to demonstrate they have certain otherwise unobservable attributes. For example, in the 1980s it was common for wealthy people to signal their wealth by driving German sports cars or sporting an alligator label on their shirts. Multinationals such as LVMH (Louis Vuitton handbags, Dom Pérignon champagne) work hard to make sure that their brands are signals of luxury in all countries.

6.5.4 Technical Standards

Technical regulations and standards set out specific characteristics of a product—such as its size, shape, design, functions and performance, or the way it is labelled or packaged before it is put on sale.
The difference between a standard and a technical regulation lies in compliance. While conformity with standards is voluntary, technical regulations are by nature mandatory.

Visit the travel store in YVR airport and you will see about 10 different types of electric plugs used in different countries. Paper sizes differ: North Americans mainly use "letter size" (8.5 by 11 inches, or 216 by 279 mm) whereas the European Union uses ISO A4 (210 by 297 mm). Keyboards in France are based on the AZERTY standard which is quite different from the QWERTY standard used in English-speaking countries. In many cases the differences are mostly arbitrary but once a standard is established, it is usually extremely costly for an individual to deviate from it. One example is the imperial system of measurements. Since the 1700s, the metric system, which is based on inter-related and generally decimal measures, has been regarded as superior. However, it has proven extremely difficult to persuade users of the imperial system to switch. Finally, the specifications for motor vehicles differ from country to country because of differences in the side of the road used for driving.

The European Commission has long considered the impact of differences in technical standards on trade within the European Union. Here I quote from a 1996 report:

> The trade-restricting impact of these national regulations barriers stems from the need to reconfigure products to comply with partner country specifications such as adjustments to packaging and labelling, registration or homologation procedures (cf. pharmaceuticals, motor vehicles, chemicals or foodstuffs) and the cost of obtaining proof, acceptable to product health and safety inspectorates in the importing country, that the product actually complies with the specifications to which it is subjected (conformity assessment).
> Technical trade barriers therefore strike at the heart of business operations, affecting pre-production, production, sales and marketing policies. The need to adapt product design, reorganise production systems, and repackage and re-test products entails costs, the magnitude of which differs across products and

technologies. The costs of producing separate national variants of lifts to meet national specifications in each of the Member States can be significant and have been estimated to add 10% to average production costs. In the automotive sector, it has been estimated that the move from separate national systems for authorisation of product models to European Whole Type Approval can lead to savings of up to 10% of the cost of model development (30 Million ECU per model). This saving does not include the scope for additional improvements arising from enhanced efficiency of production of components and assembly.

There are two important and related issues. One issue is whether product specifications are imposed by the government or by the "market." If the former, then a firm usually faces a simple choice: meet the requirements or do not sell in that nation's market. Markets do not impose standards in the same way. In some cases a firm can deviate and certain consumers will decide not to buy while others might actually prefer the deviant product. A second issue is the extent to which all consumers in a given country agree on the desired set of product specifications. If there is widespread agreement, then market determined standards will be almost as binding as regulations. Regulations differ from standards in that the former can be binding even when consumers vary in their preferred product specifications. We considered the use of regulations as disguised trade barriers in Chapter 5.

6.6 The Costs of Adaptation

There are significant costs associated with product adaptation:

Research and development costs for new varieties ("blueprints"). These costs are truly variety-specific in the sense that once they have been incurred (sunk), they need not be repeated if the same variety is manufactured in multiple locations. Note that these costs may be very low if the adaptation just involves the scaling up or down of some continuous feature such as container volume or sweetness. In other cases, adaptation involves a complete redesign. For instance a sub-compact car is not just a re-scaling of a mid-sized car.

Market cultivation costs: the market-specific advertisement and promotional pricing required to establish a new variety in a new market.

Variety-specific learning-by-doing: The more experience in producing a particular variety, the lower will be the unit costs of production.

This effect is weakened if there are big spill-overs of learning benefits from one product variety to another. For example, if most learning-by-doing in car assembly carries over in full when a firm makes a right-hand side drive car, then the cost of adaptation is low. On the other hand, when a firm introduces an engine that can run on ethanol, there will be a series of new technical problems requiring solutions. Much of the existing knowledge for gas engines no longer applies, so introducing the new type of engine involves substantial extra learning-by-doing.

Line costs: The minimum amount of machinery and workers to operate each variety's assembly line. These costs are really variety-plant pair specific. Thus, you must pay the fixed "line cost" each time you add another variety at an existing factory. Moreover, if you produce the same variety in two factories you pay the "blueprint" cost (described above) once but you pay the line cost twice.

Switching costs: Sometimes a single assembly line can be altered to produce a different variety. The "retooling" cost of changing from one variety to another on a given line is called the switching cost. These costs can sometimes be lowered if the firm adopts "flexible" machinery.

Input price rises: There are two effects. First, because there is usually a discount obtainable by purchasing in bulk, a firm that produces many varieties, each of which require different components, will experience an increase in input costs due to smaller orders. Meanwhile, input costs may rise or fall if the adaptation involves a change in *quality* of ingredients.

Consumer confusion costs: Dilution of international "identity." This is primarily important when you have customers that will sample your product in multiple locations. Then you do not want to create uncertainty about what your brand identity is. For instance, it is OK to sell a smaller version of the "Big Mac" in Japan if only Japanese will be tasting it and they will not be seeing the larger version elsewhere. However, if US customers go to Japan and find a "little Mac" they might downgrade their image of McDonalds hamburgers. This is a somewhat silly example. However, this issue may be more serious for hotels that target the international business traveler.

6.7 Weighing the Benefits and Costs

When will these costs be small enough that adaptation is the profitable decision? Generally, since most of the costs of adaptation do not increase in the number of units produced, there will be *greater incentive to adapt for a larger market.* Thus the firm will want to adapt to suit needs of citizens of big economies.

One must be careful in inferring the "size of the market" for specific products. I call this the "nobody wears shoes here" problem. The apocryphal story concerns a shoe company that sends two salesmen to different cities in a country that it has never before sold shoes. One salesman asks to return home immediately because he thinks the potential market is *zero.* After all, he reasons, "nobody wears shoes here." The other salesman requests 100,000 pairs be delivered as soon as possible since the potential market appears huge—"Nobody wears shoes here." The point is that low levels of current demand for a product may be due to the previous lack of availability of the product with the right attributes including an affordable price. If the shoe company can offer that, then there may be good reason to expect it can sell a large number of shoes. A real case of this problem lies in the difficulty of interpreting the low market share of US vehicles in Japan. Were the Japanese put off by the lack of right-hand steering models? Or was it perceived lack of quality? If the former, then current demand is a bad gauge of whether the adaptation of changing the steering position would be profitable. Thus, it is important to evaluate market size under the counterfactual assumption that the adaptation in question has been made. If using reasonable estimates of the elasticity of demand with respect to the innovation still suggests a small market, then adaptations with high fixed costs will not be worthwhile.

For a given country size, the gains from adaptation will be larger if the demand differences are (a) widespread and (b) permanent. Differences attributable to geography and climate will not change much within the firm's planning horizon and are likely to affect all consumers in a nation. Hence, it will usually pay to try to adapt to such changes.

6.8 Pricing to Market

Price is a product attribute that can be just as important as physical characteristics and branding. Like these attributes, it usually makes sense to adapt the price to suit local circumstances. "Pricing to market" is the act of determining a different price for each different market. There are several reasons why the firm might raise or lower its price relative to the home country benchmark.

1. The price should be high in markets where consumers have a *low* elasticity of demand, i.e. where demand is not very price sensitive.

2. The price should be low in markets where the firm currently takes a small share of large, homogeneous market.

3. The delivered price should be higher in markets that are far from the production site but the firm should usually absorb some of the extra freight costs. That is, FOB prices should be lower when destined to distant markets.

4. The delivered price will usually have to match the domestic competition's prices. Sometimes it is necessary to beat the local suppliers on price because they offer other advantages the foreign firm cannot match. The case of butt-weld pipe fittings is a interesting example. Imported pipe fittings were not close substitutes for domestic ones despite the similarities in the physical attributes of the products. The relevant differences were minimum order sizes ("minimum purchase amounts for all imports is generally a 40-foot container load, which typically contains fittings worth $25,000 or more, whereas domestic fittings are often sold by producers in much smaller quantities—even as little as a single fitting—and may even be shipped by expedited delivery services"), delivery time (longer for imports), product availability (certain grades, types, sizes of fittings were not available from the foreign firms), follow-up services (not typically provided by foreign firms). "Out of 301 quarterly price comparisons subject imports undersold the domestic product in 212 instances." (International Trade Commission summary report)

5. Prices should generally be set low in a new market. In marketing, charging low prices to a new market is referred to as a "market penetration" strategy. The reasoning is that customers need to be given an incentive to try unfamiliar products. Otherwise, they have a tendency to stay with the domestic products they already trust.

There are, however, constraints to the practice of price discrimination.

1. *Charging a lower price in an export market* than is charged at home can trigger a dumping investigation and result in anti-dumping duties. Indeed this happened in the pipe fittings case described above. However the duty was ultimately rejected on the grounds that the imported fittings had not caused injury to the domestic industry.

2. *Price gaps in either direction* are undermined when the good is easily transported across markets. This practice is sometimes referred to as arbitrage, although this is not a very good usage since we usually restrict that term to the case of no transaction costs. The terms "parallel trade" and "gray market" are also used.

Many firms post prices in the currency of the local market. This leads to price stability in the face of fluctuating exchange rates. Antidumping investigations compare the home market price to the export price evaluated in a common currency. Fixing prices in local currencies may therefore lead to "accidental dumping." For example, suppose that a Mexican exporter of digital cameras posts an export price for sales to the US market of $100. At that time, the exchange rate is 10 P/$. To avoid dumping allegations, the firm sets the home price at 1000 pesos. Now suppose the Peso appreciates to 9P/$. If it maintains the same posted prices, it could be accused of dumping. The reason is that the export price now stands at $P_x = 100$. The home market price, expressed in USD, is now $1000/9 = 111.11$ USD. So we see $P_x < P_n = P_H$ with a dumping margin of 11%. To avoid dumping, the exporter could repost his US export price to $111.11 or more. Alternatively, it could lower the home price to 900 Pesos—as long as that exceeds average costs of production.

References

Commission Of The European Communities, Brussels, 16.12.96 "Impact and effectiveness of the Internal Market."

Levitt, Theodore, 1983, "The Globalization of Markets" *Harvard Business Review* May/June 1983, pp. 92–102.

Shy, Oz, *The Economics of Network Industries.*

Tarantino, Quentin, *Pulp Fiction* The full text of Vincent and Jules' dialogue on Europe is available at http://www.godamongdirectors.com/scripts/pulp.shtml

Travers, Jeffrey and Stanley Milgram, 1969, "An Experimental Study of the Small World Problem," *Sociometry*, Vol. 32, No. 4. (December), pp. 425-443.

Multinational Formation

The global production strategies of multinational corporations and contractual networks are remarkably diverse. This chapter explores the range of possible multinational forms. We begin with brief descriptions of well-known multinationals that operate in very different ways. We then gradually develop a framework for analyzing the strengths and weaknesses of each form. Using this framework, we find that choosing the right form always involves a consideration of the same key issues: trade costs, plant-level economies of scale (PLEoS), market advantages, and factor advantages.

7.1 Examples of Real World Multinational Forms

Characterizing the international production structure of a firm is difficult because of the lack of public data and also that firms are continually changing their operations. In the next three subsections we contrast the operations of three well-known multinationals: Mercedes-Benz, Nestle, and Mattel.

7.1.1 Mercedes-Benz

Mercedes-Benz (MB), a unit of Daimler-Chrysler, is best known in North America as a maker of luxury cars. However, it is also a major producer of commercial vehicles (trucks). Mercedes-Benz vehicles are sold in almost every country in the world.

Mercedes originally produced all vehicles in Germany. In 1956 it started manufacturing trucks and buses in a factory in Brazil. While it continued to keep car production concentrated in Germany, MB went on to establish commercial vehicle production in seven other nations (the US, Canada, Mexico, Argentina, South Africa, Spain, and Turkey). In the early 1990s MB began producing the M class of sports-utility vehicles (SUVs) in Alabama. In 1999 Mercedes opened a new plant to make cars in a less developed country. The plant, located near Rio de Janeiro in Brazil, expanded its product line-up in 2001 from the compact A Class to also assemble the C class for the US market. The plant will be expanded to produce the Smart, which Mercedes currently makes just in Hambach, France. Around the same time, Mercedes also began to produce a right-hand-drive version of the C class in South Africa, first exporting to Australia but perhaps ultimately to the UK, Japan, Australia, New Zealand, Malta, Singapore, Malaysia, Indonesia, Thailand, Hong Kong, and Ireland.

7.1.2 Nestle's Food Products

Nestle provides a dramatic contrast to Mercedes luxury car strategy. Nestle has 508 factories in 85 nations.[1] These factories generally process locally grown farm products into locally sold food products. As shown in Table 7.1, less than 3% of Nestle's sales, factories and employees are in its home base of Switzerland.[2]

Table 7.1. Nestle's dispersed factories

Area	Shares of		
	Sales	Factories	Employees
Americas	40%	32%	41%
Europe	40%	41%	34%
(Switzerland)	(1.6%)	(1.8%)	(2.6%)
Asia, Africa & Oceania	20%	27%	25%

7.1.3 Mattel's Barbie

The Barbie doll is now 40 years old. From its inception, Barbies have been produced in Asia: first, in Japan and now in Indonesia and China. The Barbie doll makes extensive use of trade to unite its various inputs

---

[1] *2002 Management Report*

[2] Daimler-Benz on the other hand, the parent of Mercedes-Benz, has just 22% of its employment outside of Germany despite foreign markets being the source of 63% of sales.

into a final product. Barbie starts out as petroleum in the Middle East. She is then refined into plastic pellets in oil refineries in Taiwan. These pellets are melted in China and injected through molding equipment made in the US or Japan into molds made in the US. Chinese workers operate the mold injectors, add Japanese-made Nylon hair, paint details on the doll and sew Barbie's clothes from Chinese-made cotton. The financing and shipping services are provided by Hong Kong based companies. The finished doll has cost \$2 to manufacture, of which 35 cents went to Chinese workers, 65 cents to materials providers and 1 dollar to the Hong Kong managers. The doll will retail for \$10 in the US. Barbie will generate \$2 billion in revenues for Mattel through sales in 140 countries.

7.2 Multinational "Business" Strategy

Real multinationals produce many products, each of which are made from many inputs. Their operations can seem bewilderingly complex. To gain some basic insights into the decision of the best form, it is easier for us to start by considering the choices of a single-product firm. Analyses of the key decisions for a single product are sometimes referred to as *business* strategy. The location decisions of a multi-business company, referred to as *corporate* strategy, are considered in the following section.

To keep things simple, we will divide the world into two countries, Home (H) and Foreign (F). Figure 7.1 illustrates the three options available to the firm. The default position of a firm as it first serves a foreign market is "home centralization," that is to export from the home plant that is already serving the home market. A second option is to open a plant in the foreign country to serve that market while continuing to serve the home market with the original plant. We call this "replication" as it involves creating a replica of the home plant in the foreign country. The use of the replication form eliminates trade as each market is served locally.

A third option is to shut down the home plant and use a new factory in the foreign country to manufacture for both markets. This "foreign centralization" form involves importing back into the home market. Presumably some head office activities remain at home or else we would just see this as home centralization from the perspective of the foreign country. We will consider such activities in the following section but for now we want to retain the focus on a single business unit.

Home Country   **Foreign Country**

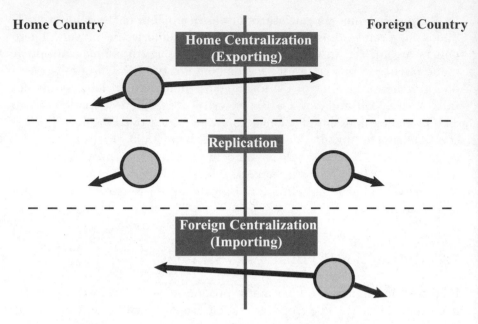

Fig. 7.1. Alternative forms for the single-product MNE

We can use a little bit of simple algebra to make our analysis more precise. We will take the size of each market as given, with there being M_H customers at home and M_F customers in the foreign country.[3]

The total cost of home centralization, C_H is given as

$$C_H = w_H M_H + (w_H + T_F) M_F + K_H,$$

where w_H is the marginal cost of home production, T_F represents the trade costs incurred in exporting to the foreign market, and M_F is the size of the foreign market, and K_H represents the fixed costs of the capital (land, buildings, equipment) deployed at the home factory. If the firm were to open another plant, it would have to incur capital costs twice (at home, K_H and in the foreign country, K_F). However, it would be able to avoid trade costs by serving markets locally. Thus the costs of replication are given by

$$C_R = w_H M_H + w_F M_F + K_H + K_F.$$

---

[3] Normally we would think the size of each market depends on the price charged, as in Chapter 6. Here we focus on costs. This can be justified if the firm is able to charge a price to each consumer equal to their willingness to pay.

Shutting down the home plant and relocating it to the foreign country can lower fixed costs to K_F, assuming that all of the home capital costs can be reversed. In reality, some structures and equipment cannot be relocated to the foreign country and do not have good alternative uses at home (i.e. they have low "salvage" value). Thus, at least in the short run some portion of K_H would still have to be incurred. Under foreign centralization, trade will become necessary again. This time trade involves the costs of importing F-made products into H, which we will denote as T_H. Therefore the costs of foreign centralization are given by

$$C_F = w_F M_F + (w_F + T_H)M_H + K_F.$$

Multinational business strategy in this example just requires us to compare C_H, C_R and C_F and select the form that yields the lowest cost.

Three-way comparisons can be complicated so we will set aside foreign centralization for the moment and consider the relative merits of home centralization (exporting) versus replication. We will also simplify things by letting $K_H = K_F = K$. Home centralization is preferred when $C_R > C_H$. This requires

$$K + w_F M_F > (w_H + T_F)M_F.$$

Note that the costs of producing for the home market have canceled each other out since both forms involve using the home factory for that market. Dividing by the size of the foreign market, M_F, we can see that exporting is preferable to replication when

$$w_F + K/M_F > w_H + T_F.$$

Figure 7.2 graphs the left and right hand sides of the inequality. It shows that replicating overseas investment can only be justified when the foreign market is large enough.

We can solve for the critical market size required to justify replicating investment. This is the $\hat{M}_F$ that sets $C_H = C_R$:

$$\hat{M}_F = \frac{K}{T_F - (w_F - w_H)}$$

The numerator, K, tells us the importance of *scale economies*. The larger are scale economies the larger will the foreign market have to be to justify the additional fixed costs of setting up a new factory overseas. In the denominator, we see first *trade costs*. The bigger they are, the smaller the critical size of the foreign market. In parentheses in the denominator we see the home country's *factor advantage* (when

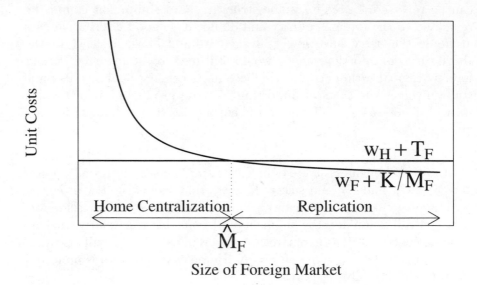

Fig. 7.2. The critical foreign market size to justify replicating investment

positive). The larger the home factor advantage the bigger the foreign market will have to be to justify replicating investment.

Another way to frame the decision is to focus on the distance between the countries. Recall that trade costs to reach the foreign market are given by the sum of the costs created by the foreign border, B_F, and the distance cost. The latter depends on the cost per kilometer d multiplied by the total distance to the foreign market, D_F. Thus, trade costs to reach the foreign market are given by

$$T_F = B_F + dD_F,$$

In Figure 7.3 we hold the amount to be sold in a foreign market constant and graph the costs of exporting versus replication as function of distance to the foreign market.

Increases in trade costs parameters (B and d) and decreases in scale economies parameters (K) make the firm more inclined to produce overseas, i.e. it will do so at shorter distances and for smaller markets.

Now we must consider the third option: foreign centralization. In doing so we will focus on the share of the world market ($M_H + M_F$) in each country. The letter m represents the home country's share of

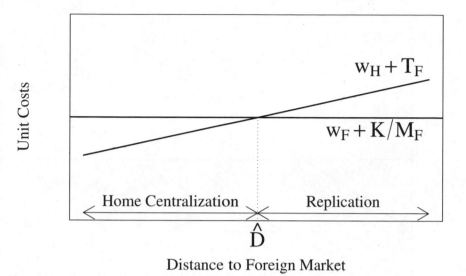

Fig. 7.3. The critical distance to the foreign market to justify replicating investment

world demand, that is $m = M_H/(M_H + M_F)$. Dividing all the costs by total production we obtain the following unit cost equations:

$$c_H = C_H/(M_H + M_F) = w_H + T_F(1 - m) + K/(M_H + M_F)$$

$$c_R = C_R/(M_H + M_F) = w_H m + w_F(1 - m) + 2K/(M_H + M_F)$$

$$c_F = C_F/(M_H + M_F) = w_F + T_H m + K/(M_H + M_F)$$

Figure 7.4 graphs the costs of each form against the share of demand in the home country. Home centralization yields low costs when the home country market is relatively large. Conversely, foreign centralization makes sense when the home market is small. Replication looks good when the markets are about the same size. The figure is drawn for the case where there are no factor advantages, that is $w_H = w_F$.

7.3 Combining the Four Elements

The algebra in the proceeding section is useful because it forces us to be very precise about our assumptions. For those uncomfortable with

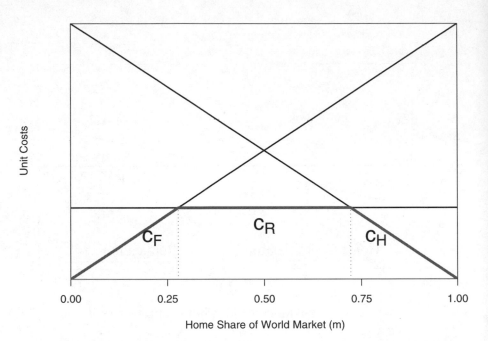

Fig. 7.4. The low-cost form depends on the home country's share of world demand

algebra, it may be confusing. Hence, it is worth restating in words the key concepts and how they influence the decision between multinational forms.

Start with *factor advantages*. The home country has a factor advantage when $w_F > w_H$, that is when the costs of (productivity-adjusted) factors are higher in the foreign country. The key idea is that when the intensively used factors are relatively abundant or relatively productive at home, then home centralization (exporting) will tend to be the preferred form. Replication looks better when factor abundances at home and overseas are similar, that is $w_F \approx w_H$. In that case, we do not have to worry about producing in a place with the wrong factor advantages.

Next, consider *trade costs*. The higher are trade costs (T in the algebra), the more important it is to avoid them by producing in the same country where the product will be consumed. This is sometimes referred to as a "proximity" advantage. Large distances between countries favor the replication form. High border effects also raise the attractiveness of replication but one must also pay attention to *which* border is costly to cross. If only the home country imposes high border costs, then home centralization starts to look relatively good.

The reduction in trade costs caused by replication comes at the costs of bearing more fixed costs, that is a loss of scale economies. Average production costs rise when the MNE does the "same thing" in two different locations. This is due to the failure to exploit plant-level economies of scale (PLEoS). The opportunity to exploit scale economies in the algebra of the previous section was captured in K, the plant-specific fixed costs. The K represents the minimum, *indivisible* amount of capital administrative labour costs required to produce any output at all. When a minimum fixed level of capital or labour must be deployed in order to produce any positive level of output in a location, there will be PLEoS associated with spreading the fixed costs across large amounts of output. As described in Chapter 2, a second source of PLEoS is *geometric cost-capacity relationships*. These primarily affect industries that use some kind of container in production. In addition to the static PLEoS—where average costs depend on *current* output at the plant—there are also dynamic PLEoS. Plant-specific learning-by-doing causes average costs to depend on the *cumulative* production carried out at a plant.

Scale economies are less important when plants are subject to binding *capacity* constraints. This is the case where it becomes extremely costly as the firm tries to expand production at a given location above its operating capacity. We may visualize capacity constraints as regions where the average cost curve rises sharply with output.

In summary, scale economies are large when there are substantial plant-level indivisibilities (or quasi-fixed costs), engineering economies, plant-level learning by doing, and capacity constraints do not bind.

Scale economies strongly favor *centralization somewhere*. Home centralization will tend to win out relative to foreign centralization when there are home factor advantages or high home border costs. Also if a large share of home capital costs are already sunk, this will make foreign centralization less attractive. Location-specific learning-by-doing is a case where the scale economy is sunk because one cannot relocate or sell off the tacit knowledge derived from production experience in a location. Thus dynamic scale economies usually favor home centralization. The exception is for a new product where there has been no learning-by-doing yet. This puts foreign centralization back on a level playing field with home centralization.

The final element to multinational strategy is the issue of the international distribution of demand, or *market sizes*. When one market is much larger than the other and that market imposes relatively high border effects then it will be a good candidate location for centralization. When both markets are large, replication is advantageous.

As we consider more complex multinational forms in the next section or when we evaluate forms adopted by real-world multinationals, remember that the right form always depends on these four elements of multinational strategy: factor advantages, trade costs, scale economies, and market sizes.

7.4 Multinational Corporate Strategy

In the previous section we considered where to locate a single product. In fact, most MNEs produce many products (we use the term "product" to refer to any production activity, whether it is a tangible good or a service). If these products are *unrelated* then corporate strategy is just repeated application of business strategy. That is one evaluates each business deciding between the three forms of home centralization, foreign centralization, and replication. An example of a firm that appears to produce essentially unrelated products would be Yamaha with its stereo speakers, pianos, and motorcycles.

Multinational corporate strategy becomes interesting when firms produce related products. The two most basic relations between products are vertical and horizontal. The former corresponds to the case of intermediate products used to create final products. The latter corresponds to sets of final products.

7.4.1 Forms for Two Vertically Related Products

Most goods and services are produced through a sequence of activities, or stages. To address this issue while still keeping things as simple as possible, we consider only two products, "U" for *upstream* and "D" for *downstream*. Since real production processes generally involve more than two vertically related products, we have to judiciously lump products together to create our U and D. Consider five examples taken from manufacturing and services:

- Steel: U is the blast furnace, D combines the steel furnace and rolling mill.
- Oil: U combines exploration and production of crude, D combines refining and distribution of gasoline and petrochemicals.
- Autos: U combines chassis, body panels, and electronics, D is the assembly of the parts into finished vehicles.

- Movies: U is scripting, filming, and editing, D is exhibition to audiences.
- Teaching: U is preparation of lectures and exams, D is presentation of lectures and evaluation of student performance.

All the possible forms for a home-based firm are shown in Figure 7.5. Here we define the home base using the location of the upstream product. There are additional possibilities not shown in the figure for foreign-based forms. The thin arrows represent flows of intermediate inputs from upstream to downstream units, while the thick arrows show shipments of final products from the downstream plant to final consumers.

The following bullet lists contain some rules of thumb about conditions that make each of the primary forms more attractive. In general, the firm will have to weigh the relative strengths of each advantage and disadvantage to reach a final decision on the right form.

Choose a *Centralization* form when

- plant-level scale economies are important for both products,
- trade costs are large for the upstream product,
- trade costs are low on the downstream product.
- The home base is the major market, i.e. foreign countries have low demand for the final product,
- the home base offers factor advantages for both the upstream and downstream products.

Choose a *Replication* form when

- trade costs are high both on upstream and downstream products,
- scale economies are small: plant-level fixed costs and opportunities for plant-level learning-by-doing are not very large relative to the sizes of markets,
- countries do not have strong factor advantages in either product, presumably because the two countries have similar relative factor abundances.

Choose a *Specialization* form when

- different countries have important factor advantages that differ across the two products (upstream has different factor intensities from downstream and the home country has different factor abundances from the foreign country).
- all trade costs are low,
- there are high scale economies for each product.

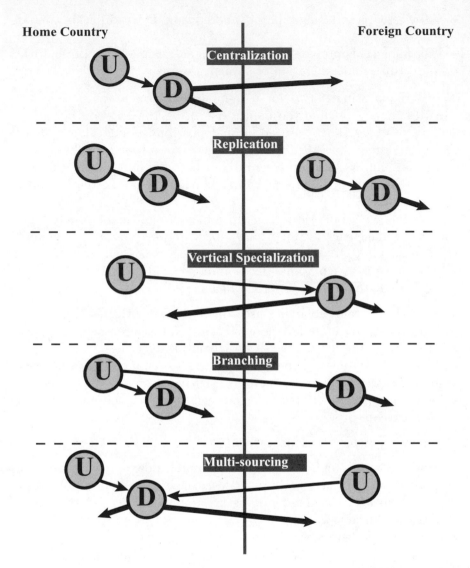

Fig. 7.5. Alternative forms for vertically-related 2-product MNEs

Note that there may be a conflict such that each form has advantages and disadvantages. In that case it may be preferable to use a blend.

Figure 7.5 shows two "blends" in which the firm replicates one stage and centralizes the other. The first and most common is the *branching* form. The branching firm is worried about the trade costs involved in reaching its final consumers. Hence it moves just the downstream product to the foreign markets. Thus it is replicating, but only the downstream product.

The branching form might be a first step towards replicating both products. Indeed, most multinationals grew according to a fairly regular pattern. They started producing solely for the domestic market, using mostly domestic inputs. Then they began to export using foreign agents as distributors. Next they started sales offices in their major markets. Then they followed with final assembly in major markets and sales offices in secondary markets. The assembly plants would initially rely on headquarters for components and support services. The move to replication would involve adding upstream capacity in each market. However the firm might want to stop at the branching form. The reason is that there may be large economies of scale in upstream products like engineering, design, strategic management, and the manufacture of core components. These scale economies argue against full replication.

As a concrete example, suppose that the key component of a car that distinguishes it from its competitors is the engine. Suppose also that manufacture and design of engines should be done in the same place, so that there can be fast and frequent feedback between designers and plant managers. Suppose further that tariffs on engines are not very high but tariffs on finished autos are very high. Then it makes sense to centralize design and manufacture of engines at the headquarters and decentralize assembly to the foreign markets.

The strategy of retaining key upstream production and support services in the home country is often viewed negatively by the countries that are hosts to final assembly and distribution. They refer to the plants they host as "screwdriver" factories because workers there simply put things together, adding relatively little value to the product.

A second type of blend is shown in the bottom frame of Figure 7.5. This one is less common and has no established name—I call it "multi-sourcing." This form is somewhat strange since, at face value, it appears to combine a number of disadvantages. Final production must be exported to the foreign market and intermediates are imported from the foreign market. These extra trade costs lower profits. Upstream production occurs in two countries involving a loss of scale economies.

Moreover, since only one of the two countries will have a factor advantage in the upstream product, there is a question of why the firm would bother to produce in the other location.

A simple reason for multi-sourcing is if each individual upstream unit does not have sufficient production capacity to satisfy the whole needs of the downstream unit. Thus an oil refinery might well import crude oil from wells in several oil producing nations. Capacity constraints act to sharply reduce scale economies. However, this would appear to be a short-run problem. Over time one would expect the multinational to expand capacity in whichever country had a factor advantage or just in the country hosting the downstream plant if trade costs were an overwhelming consideration.

A motive for long run use of a multi-sourcing form could be flexibility in the face of an uncertain future business environment. At any given point in time one country or another will have a factor advantage. However, if economic conditions change, there may be a switch in which country is the low-cost producer for the upstream product. If these changes occur at a rapid pace, perhaps due to real exchange rate appreciation, there may not be time to relocate upstream production. Instead, the firm maintains factories in both countries and will tend to have excess capacity in the country that has lost factor advantage while it runs its low cost factory at full speed.

Another interpretation is that the upstream product consists of two different and complementary inputs. In that case, the firm sources each of them from the country with a factor advantage. While realistic, this explanation runs counter to our working assumption of a single upstream product and a single downstream product.

To summarize, the firm should choose the *branching* form when

- trade costs are high on downstream products and low on upstream products.
- scale economies for downstream are small but high on upstream.
- the home country has a factor advantage in upstream.
- Neither country has a strong factor advantage in downstream products.

Choose the *multi-sourcing* form when

- scale economies for downstream are high but there are diseconomies of scale for upstream products, perhaps due to binding capacity constraints or due to desire to insure against country-specific shocks.
- trade costs for all products are small.
- the home country has a factor advantage in downstream products.

- neither country has a strong factor advantage in upstream products.

Figure 7.5 considered only two-country forms. With more than two countries, there are many more possible forms. For instance, one possibility is to produce the upstream product at home and the downstream stage in a country near a major market which is reached by exporting. For instance, Sony might opt to make cathode ray tubes (CRTs) in Japan for export to Mexico where they are assembled (with other inputs) into television sets (TVs) which are primarily exported to the United States.[4] Ireland is a popular location for factories that use inputs from US headquarters to assemble goods to be sold in the rest of the European Union. We might call this the "boomerang" form since inputs make an "arc" through an intermediate assembly country on their way to the final consumer.

7.4.2 Three Product Forms

Let us now continue to have vertically related products in a two-country world but add a second downstream product. The two downstream products are called "D1" and "D2." In contrast to "U" and "D" which are *vertically* related, "D1" and "D2" are *horizontally* related.

Figure 7.6 illustrates a number of multinational forms for a three-product enterprise. The first three frames of the figure all maintain upstream units in the same country as downstream units. Implicitly, then, we have assumed high trade costs relative to scale economies for the upstream product. We consider the alternative case in the final two frames of the figure.

The "monocentric" form corresponds to the centralization form shown in Figure 7.5. Everything is done in the home country and the foreign market is reached by exporting. By contrast, the "polycentric" and "polymorphic" forms resemble the replication form shown in Figure 7.5 in that upstream and downstream products are done in each country. The subsidiaries are not true "replicas" of each other, though, since they produce different final products. The "polycentric" form centralizes production of each final good in a *different* country and then offers a full menu of products to consumers in each country by importing the non-local product. This approach sometimes goes by the name of "world product mandates" since each national subsidiary has a mandate to manufacture its product from scratch and then sell it to the

---

[4] In fact, I believe Sony makes the CRTs used in its Tijuana TV factories in San Diego.

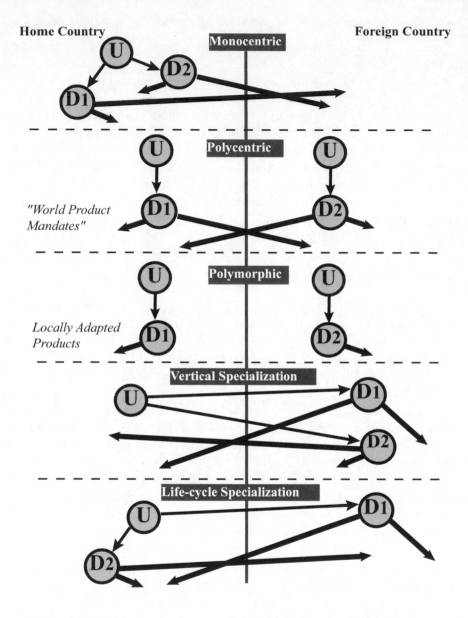

Fig. 7.6. Alternative forms for two-stage MNEs with two final products

world market. In a multi-country setting, firms might only give a particular subsidiary a "regional mandate" (e.g. Western Europe or North America). The "polymorphic" form has the same geographic allocation of activities as the polycentric form but a different pattern of final shipments. Like the replication form from Figure 7.5, the polymorphic form involves no cross-border trade.

The decision between the monocentric, polycentric, and polymorphic forms depends in large part on the nature of the relationship between the downstream final products. There are three special cases of horizontally related products:

- *Joint Outputs:* products that are created at more or less the same time as the result of a single basic activity. These arise when production of one good makes it very inexpensive (or free) to produce another good. Examples include beef and leather that are joint outputs of the slaughter of cattle, the lumber, sawdust and chips produced at sawmills, and gasoline and other petro-chemicals produced at oil refineries.
- *Substitutes:* products having similar attributes and functions. Consumers see each product as alternative means of satisfying the same basic wants. Examples include breweries like Anheuser-Busch with its Lite, Busch, Budweiser, and Michelob beers and car companies that manufacture minivans and sports utility vehicles (SUVs).
- *Complements:* products that are used together by the customer. Rather than fulfilling the same purpose, these products assist each other in accomplishing a goal. Gillette is a good example, with its razors, shaving cream, and after-shave lotion. Other examples would include tractors and trailers, amplifiers and electric guitars.

In the case of joint outputs, *inter-product* trade costs are usually very high. Indeed, in the sawmill case it is not technically feasible to geographically separate the generation of chips, boards, and sawdust. This suggests a monocentric form, although full replication (not shown) of all three activities would also work. The optimal decision depends on trade costs with respect to reaching final customers and scale economies from consolidating production in one location.

In contrast with joint outputs, the relationship between complements and substitutes occurs on the demand side. Hence, the polycentric form remains a feasible option. The polycentric form may be preferred to centralization if trade costs are moderately high but not insurmountable and both countries have large markets. In that case, polycentrism ensures that consumers in each market have access to a locally produced product. The particular configuration we have shown performs especially well if consumers in the foreign country have a particular preference for D2 whereas those in the home country prefer D1. The more different preferences are, the greater the benefit of polycentrism relative to monocentrism *if* trade costs are significant for final goods. In the absence of high trade costs, it is important to remember that the firm need not produce locally to be responsive to local tastes. It can engage in monocentrism but mainly ship D2 to the foreign country. This would avoid unnecessary replication of upstream activities. If, on the other hand, trade costs are very high and preferences very different, then the MNE may elect to simply stop trading and move to the polymorphic form shown in the third frame.

The polymorphic and polycentric forms have advantages over the full replication form shown in figure 7.5. If the firm's use of replication is a response to high tariffs or transport costs, it will have an assembly factory in each country anyway. As a result, it may not add much to costs to have that factory produce a model that is well adapted to local tastes. This presumes that the main cost of adding an extra product lies in adding another assembly line to a factory (line costs). On the other hand, if the firm would have to undertake R&D to develop the new product (blueprint costs), then those costs would be born no matter where the product ultimately ends up being manufactured.

Consider a firm that starts out as a single-product centralist. What happens if (a) trade costs rise on final goods, or (b) the size of the foreign market increases? In both cases, we know from figures 7.3 and 7.2 that the firm will have an incentive to invest in the foreign country. Given that it is investing anyway, it might as well manufacture a product for the foreign country that is well-adapted to its tastes.

Local production does not always lead to polymorphism. Indeed, while McDonalds and Coca Cola make minor adjustments to accommodate variation in local tastes, they offer essentially the same product worldwide, even though it is almost always produced by their "branch plants" (franchise-restaurants and bottling plants). Thus standardized replication is not only possible, it often appears profitable. This will be the case when blueprint costs are high relative to line costs and trade costs (for McDonald's the perishability of the Big Mac and for Coca Cola the weight, bulk and fragility of bottled drinks) are high.

Reductions in trade costs might lead to more single-product centralization. This need not always be the case, though. Suppose the firm starts out replicating both products in each country. As trade costs fall, it might opt to continue to offer both products but centralize each of them in a different country. Polycentrism is likely to be profitable relative to monocentrism when D1 and D2 have different factor advantages. The more different are the firm's products in their factor intensities, the more likely there will be important factor advantages to be gained by placing production in different countries. Note, however, that if the countries have very different factor proportions then it does not make a lot of sense to carry out U in both places since one place is likely to have a strong factor advantage in U. This leads us to consider forms that separate U from one or both of the downstream units.

The "vertical specialization" form shown here is essentially the same as the one shown in figure 7.5. In both cases the presumption is that home has a factor advantage in upstream activities and foreign has the factor advantage in downstream. This would certainly make sense for cases like plastic products where the downstream molding and assembly and packaging are likely to make intensive use of unskilled labour whereas the upstream refining of crude oil into plastic pellets is much more capital intensive. In other cases, it may be that one of the products has more in common with upstream than it does with the other final product. Imagine that D1 and D2 have the same basic function but different levels of technical sophistication (for example D1 could be black and white TV and D2 could be colour, or D1 could be a 100mg Zip disk and D2 could be a 250mg Zip disk). Suppose further that U consists of the design and engineering of both products. Then U and D2 might be skilled-labour intensive relative to D1. Due to standardization of D1, there may be less need for frequent communication between U and D1 and hence lower intra-firm trade costs. This could easily lead to a situation in which "first-generation" D1 products are produced in a country with a relative abundance of low-skilled workers and a population of consumers that can only afford low-sophistication products. Second-generation D2 products would be produced in countries that had higher relative abundance of skilled workers and larger average purchasing power of the customers. Nevertheless, D2 products could be exported to the country producing D1 products to serve an affluent minority of customers there. The final frame in figure 7.6 illustrates this form and titles it "life-cycle specialization" in reference to the international product life-cycle that it resembles. By keeping U (product invention), D2 (cutting edge product manufacturing) close together, it puts product developers and manufacturers geographically close to the consumers.

7.5 Revisiting the Exemplars

Until recently Mercedes used the centralization form for its cars. Even today the non-German car factories account for a very small share of its total car production. Mercedes' use of home centralization cannot be explained by the absence of transportation costs or tariffs. Cars are fairly expensive to transport and subject to large tariffs in many countries. In fact, most of the world's major car companies have established factories in each of their major markets. This has not been the case for makers of *luxury* cars, where makers seem to follow Mercedes in employing the centralization form. This suggests that the reputation for high quality is tied to production in the home country. In the case of Mercedes the key asset seems to be "German Engineering." Indeed it may be that Germany has a comparative advantage in the luxury car industry. That is despite high wages, the skills in engineering are even higher.

Why can't German engineering be carried out at overseas plants? It appears that internal communication costs make the transfer of engineering skill difficult. Furthermore, even if it could be done, it would be necessary to communicate to final customers that an S-Class luxury car made in the US is just as valuable as one made in Germany. This might be a difficult task. Another way of thinking about this is that there is a large amount of location-specific (non-transferable) learning by doing involved in making luxury cars. Thus it might be prohibitively costly to replicate that learning at a new site.

At the same time as Mercedes-Benz continues to follow a centralization form in the luxury car segment, it has been increasingly dispersing its truck production to overseas markets. Since it still only manufactures in a small share of the markets in which it sells, we would not describe the current situation as a replication form, but rather as a blend. However, the foreign subsidiaries make some of their own parts and have developed their own product design and engineering staffs. Why would the same company use entirely different forms for seemingly similar products? Probably there are fewer economies of scale in commercial vehicle production.

Nestle is a replicator. A replication form in food products makes some sense. First of all, food is difficult to transport because it tends to be bulky and, more importantly, perishable. Second, some of the largest trade barriers are found on agricultural products including even processed foods. Furthermore tastes often differ from country to country based on what has traditionally been locally plentiful. These taste differences make it difficult to manufacture a single product in one country and export it to multiple markets. On the other hand, food factories do not appear to have large scale economies. This can be seen, for instance in the fact that Nestle has 12 factories each in relatively small markets such as Canada and South Africa. Thus high trade costs, products adapted to local factor advantages, and unimportant scale economies, combine to make the Replication form appropriate for Nestle.

As trade barriers decline in some areas, Nestle appears ready to move towards greater use of of the polycentric form. Thus in Europe, it makes Buitoni brand pizza in France, Buitoni brand pasta in Italy and ships both products to both countries as well as Nestle's home market, Switzerland.[5]

Barbie is made using a Specialization Strategy to take advantage of the fact that the activities involved in her manufacture have very different country costs. Labour intensive tasks such as painting and sewing have low country costs in low wage nations. Refining oil or creating expensive machinery is capital and technology intensive. Therefore less developed countries are unlikely to have a cost advantage in those activities. Finally the oil itself comes from countries with the crucial natural resource endowments.

Note that while country costs are the primary determinant of the location of production, there is some evidence for a role for trade costs. First, while most dolls obtain their hair from Italian factories, Barbie gets hers from nearer by Japan. Similarly, there are many oil refining nations but few as close as Taiwan. Overall, though, Barbie and her inputs seem to be relatively cheap to transport.

Finally, there appear to be some plant-level economies of scale in toy-making. Barbie's Chinese factories employ 5,500 workers, nearly four times as many as in Mercedes Benz' SUV plant in Alabama.

References

Steinmetz, Greg and Tara Parker-Pope, "Nestle: All Over the Map," *The Wall Street Journal* September 26, 1996.

Rone Tempest, "Barbie and the World Economy" *Los Angeles Times* September 22, 1996.

Rosenzweig, Philip, "Mercedes Benz" Harvard Business School Case 9-394-084.

---

[5] I draw this example from a recent paper by Richard Baldwin and Gianmarco Ottaviano.

8

Internalization

This chapter takes up the question of how to organize overseas business. The first question is why do firms ever wish to *own* assets and employ workers in foreign countries. You might think the answer is obvious. If you want to produce abroad, then don't you have to invest abroad? As a matter of fact, you do not. All of Nike's shoes and most of McDonald's hamburgers are made abroad by independently owned firms. Of the many tasks involved in delivering final products to consumers, which should be done in-house and which should be outsourced? The decision of how a firm should draw its organizational boundaries is a critical question for domestic strategy and even more important for multinational strategy. We will start with the general issue of the most appropriate scope of activities to be brought under the roof of a single firm. We then turn to the question of how international borders between nations affect the drawing of the firm's corporate boundaries.

8.1 Asset Heavy or Asset Light?

Henry Ford had a big idea. He wanted his company to start with raw materials (iron ore, coal, limestone, rubber trees, and even soy beans!) and turn them into finished automobiles. There would be no other companies standing between natural resources and consumers. In practice, Ford was never 100% self-sufficient. However, it seems unlikely that any company ever came as close to perfect vertical integration. The embodiment of this idea was the River Rouge "multiplex." With over a 100,000 employees spread across 2,000 acres, it was the largest industrial facility in the world.

There were docks, steel furnaces, coke ovens, rolling mills, glass furnaces and plate-glass rollers. Buildings included a tire-

making plant, stamping plant, engine casting plant, frame and
assembly plant, transmission plant, radiator plant, tool and die
plant, and at one time, even a paper mill. A massive power plant
produced enough electricity to light a city the size of nearby
Detroit, and a soybean conversion plant turned soybeans into
plastic auto parts.
http://www.hfmgv.org/rouge/history.asp

Beyond the River Rouge facility, Ford owned 700,000 acres of forest,
iron ore mines and limestone quarries, even a rubber tree plantation in
Brazil. The railroads and ships used to transport these inputs to River
Rouge also belonged to Ford.

Today most of Ford's non-automotive assets have been closed or
sold. There are still six manufacturing plants spread across 600 acres at
River Rouge but employment has fallen to 6,000. Ford's big idea—what
we can call the "asset-heavy strategy"—has been largely abandoned.

Jeffrey Skilling had a very different idea, shaped during his years
at the McKinsey Consulting firm. Skilling's big idea was embodied in
the trading rooms of the company he ran: Enron. Before he became
infamous for his role in the collapse that company, he was celebrated
for transforming Enron with his "asset-light strategy." Enron grew at
what seemed to be spectacular rates once it moved away from asset-
heavy businesses, such as power generation in India, to trading energy
contracts (and later weather derivatives and broadband).

Mr. Skilling believed that deregulation and market forces would
force traditional, asset-heavy companies to break up into thousands of niche players. Rather than being vertically integrated,
companies would be "virtually integrated"–by enterprises such
as Enron that would "wire those thousands of firms back together cheaply and temporarily."
The Economist December 6th, 2001.

There are two broad types of asset-light strategies. In the most extreme form that Enron seemed to embrace, the firm does not make
things; it makes deals. This requires little more in the way of physical assets than a trading room and lots of computers. For firms that
actually make "things," the second asset-light strategy is to sell off non-
core assets so as to specialize in one very narrow range of activities.

In Skilling's vision, such specialist firms would be linked to the related firms via trading companies like Enron.[1]

Underlying the big ideas of Ford and Skilling are two contrasting views of arms-length transactions. The Fordist view is skeptical of the ability of markets to coordinate productive activities and relies on centralized command from corporate headquarters. The Skilling view is optimistic that markets can allow for much greater decentralization. If Ford were right, multinationals should always strive to own the producers of their foreign inputs. They should also own the firms that distribute their products abroad. If Skilling is right, there is no real need for multinationals at all. Each firm could stay in one place and be linked to everyone else it might buy or sell to via intermediaries such as the Enron trading room. So who's right? You may not be surprised that I will argue for a middle road involving a mixed use of ownership and contractual relationships.

8.2 Organizing Business Relationships

There are a number of ways to organize the producers of intermediate goods and services and the firms that purchase from them, engage in further processing, and sell to downstream firms or final consumers.

Spot transactions: Arm's length arrangements in which cash and commodities (or services) are swapped on the "spot." Thus the two parties to the transaction have no long-term relationship at all.

Long-term contracting: Legal agreements including alliances, supply networks, and agency relationships. An alliance is a long-term arrangement between firms that might otherwise be competing with each other that is more closely involved than a normal "spot market" transaction but that does not go so far as to merge the firms into a single entity. When a single firm engages in a set of long-term purchasing relationships with a large set of suppliers or distributors, we often call the resulting group a *network*.

Ownership: vertical or horizontal "integration." This is also called *internalization* since it brings two otherwise separate entities together to become one firm. The control of assets used for upstream and downstream activities is centralized under management appointed by the owners of the commonly-owned assets.

---

[1] I have to admit here that I have not actually read Skilling's own account of this vision. I am not even sure it exists. Instead, I have pieced it together from articles and books on Enron, as well as articles published by McKinsey.

Each of these modes of coordination has advantages but each also has important drawbacks.

8.3 Problems with Spot Transactions

Spot transactions involve a commodity that is sold for cash and delivered immediately. These sort of markets occupy a central position in economics. One important idea is that the "invisible hand" will lead to efficient outcomes without centralized control. Spot markets work well when there is ample competition on both sides, i.e. many buyers and many sellers.

8.3.1 Relationship-Specific Investment

Williamson (1975) showed how "relationship-specific investment" (RSI) can lead to ex-post monopoly power. An investment is deemed specific to a relationship when the asset it creates is of lesser value to parties outside the relationship. For example, suppose an auto parts supplier builds a plant in Toyota City, Japan. Suppose, realistically, that to take the plant apart and reconstruct it elsewhere would be extremely expensive. Furthermore accept that the cost of transporting parts within Japan is very costly, particularly due to the use of the just-in-time (JIT) inventory system. Under these assumptions the plant in Toyota City is an RSI: it is much more valuable deployed in the relationship with Toyota than it would be with Honda.

RSI is generally beneficial for both partners in the relationship. It has the unfortunate consequence, however, of creating the "hold- up" problem, also known as "opportunistic" behaviour. Returning to our example of the parts supplier, its decision to locate in Toyota City has rendered it vulnerable to Toyota. The assembler, recognizing that the supplier has chosen a location that makes it difficult to sell to other car makers might demand a 10% price cut. What can the supplier do other than concede? It no longer has a credible option to sell to other assemblers. In other words, it is *captive*. Fear of opportunism might even prevent the formation of the Toyota City supplier cluster. This would raise costs for Toyota. Is there any way to resolve this problem? Fortunately, there are several. The obvious way is for Toyota to make its own parts, i.e. purchase the parts supplier. Now the profits of the supplier are profits of Toyota. There is no reason to exploit yourself! Thus we see that RSI plus opportunism create an incentive to internalize, i.e. to bring assembly and parts manufacture into the same corporation.

Internalization is not the only option. A simple alternative is contracting. Toyota can write a contract with the supplier that commits Toyota in advance to a certain price. Penalties for breach of contract then provide the incentive not to engage in opportunistic behaviour. Instead of an explicit contract, Toyota might opt for an *implicit* contract, i.e. one that is not specified in paper but rather is "understood" by all parties involved. Toyota knows that business is not a "one-shot game." Other firms will learn how Toyota treats its suppliers. No one will want to deal with a known opportunist. Thus, Toyota has incentive to build and maintain a *reputation* as an honest and reliable partner in its relationships.

8.3.2 Downstream Incentive Problems

As firms internationalize, one of the first decisions they face is whether to distribute their product overseas through an independent agent or own their own distribution branch in the target market. Even veterans of international expansion reevaluate this decision from time to time.

Consider the case of Coca Cola. In virtually every market Coke makes its money by selling "concentrate" to independent firms that bottle the soft drinks and then distribute them to retailers. Gross margins on concentrate are roughly 85% of sales.[2] Pernod-Ricard, primarily a maker of alcoholic beverages, owned the bottling and distribution rights for Coke in France. In the late 1980s Coke began to question this arrangement. Coca Cola seemed to be under-performing in Europe in general and France in particular. Fourth among commercial beverages in Europe (after coffee, milk and beer), per capita consumption was 30% of the US level where soft drinks are number one. And France had the lowest per capita consumption in the EU.

Coke felt the problem was one of poor marketing performance by Pernod. There were two main problems: high price and low promotion. The root sources of the problems could be viewed as *externalities*. If it promoted Coke (or Fanta Orange which it also bottled), Pernod might reduce sales of substitute products of its own manufacture, namely Orangina. Thus by lax promotion of Coke products, Pernod may have increased its own aggregate profits at the expense of Coca Cola Corporation's profits. We refer to this as a *moral hazard* problem.

---

[2] The information and quotes used in this example were derived from "Coke gets off its can in Europe," by Patricia Sellers in *Fortune*, 8/13/90.

Second, even if it had not manufactured competitor products, Pernod would not have had the right incentives to market Coke. The reason is that on each dollar of extra sales, Pernod kept less than 15 cents whereas Coca Cola received 85 cents. Thus, this positive externality implies that Pernod does not see the whole benefit of its marketing effort and hence will tend to under-supply promotion and overprice the final product. The problem of the distributor charging a price that is too high to maximize total profits is called *double marginalization.*

Coke forced Pernod to sell back the bottling and distribution rights for $140m. Then it sent William Hoffman, a successful Atlanta bottler, to France to promote Coca Cola sales. Hoffman began quarterly meetings with the heads of 11 major grocery chains. He encouraged them to lower their prices, arguing that lower margins could yield higher profits through large increases in sales (He had managed to double Coke consumption per capita in his previous job). He also extolled the virtues of large and flashy displays.

> In less than a year he has hired 500 new employees (10,000 applied), including 350 "merchandisers" who visit 15,000 retail outlets every month and make sure the Coke is properly presented. A licensed helicopter pilot and a lieutenant colonel in the U.S. Army Reserves, Hoffman has equipped his troops for battle: They wear uniforms and carry kits that include a tape measure (to measure shelves and displays), a disposable camera (to photograph them), a feather duster, and Windex (to keep them clean). In the new Coca Cola University training program, recruits take written exams on merchandising. They receive pay raises when they pass and rewards like trips to Miami when they build world-beating store displays.

8.3.3 Information Transfer

Selling information is quite different from selling most commodities. If you are thinking about buying a house that is for sale, you are free to visit the house and have it inspected and appraised prior to making the purchase. After thorough analysis, if you think the price is too high, then you can opt not to buy. No harm (other than the cost of the inspection) is done to either party. On the contrary, if I want to sell you an idea, I face a severe problem. If I tell you nothing about the idea, you probably are not willing to pay much. On the other hand, if I tell you enough about the idea to allow you to adequately assess its value, then you may know enough to take advantage of the idea without paying the price I am asking. Unlike the case of the house, it is very difficult for me to prevent you from benefiting from an idea that you did not pay for. This point is illustrated in a 1998 movie called *The Spanish Prisoner*. In that movie, the protagonist has invented something called "The Process." The firm possessing The Process is promised a "dominant market share." But what exactly is The Process? No one knows. The formulas are kept in a safe until the sale is made. Will the protagonist be compensated for his invention or will the idea be stolen?

A major concern of the licensor of a new product or process he has invented is whether the licensee, once in possession of the technology, will become a competitor for the licensor. This threat can often be handled in contracts through "non-compete" clauses. This enables Anheuser-Busch to license its beer to be made in Canada by Labatt without being particularly worried that Labatt will start selling a Budweiser clone in the United States.

The importance of information transfer problems in international business is described in the following quote by Holmstrom and Roberts (1998):

> Two organizations that we have studied in the development and transfer of knowledge are particularly central are ABB, Asea Brown Boveri, the largest electrical equipment manufacturer, and British Petroleum, the fourth-largest integrated oil company. Both firms see the opportunity to learn and share information effectively as key to their competitive advantage, and both operate with extremely lean headquarters that are too small to play a central, direct role in transferring knowledge across units. ABB spends a huge amount of time and effort sharing technical and business information across its more than 1,300 business units around the world through a variety of mechanisms. This would hardly be possible if these businesses were not under the single ABB umbrella. Similarly, BP's 100 business units have been encouraged to share information extensively through "peer assists," which involve business units calling on people from other units to help solve operating problems. BP also has a network of different "federal groups," each of which encourages technologists and managers from units around the world to share knowledge about similar challenges that they face.

The idea is that information within a firm can be thought of as a public good. Headquarters wants to make sure the information is used as broadly as possible.

8.3.4 Reputation Transfer

Knowledge is not the only intangible asset that is difficult to transfer through market transactions. Reputation for providing high quality goods or services forms the basis of success for many MNEs. Examples of industries where reputation is important include auditing firms, consultancies, hotels, and drugs (both legal and illegal). The exact nature of the reputation problem differs from industry to industry but it typically works as follows. Consumers are willing to pay more if they believe the firm is supplying high-quality products. But the producer is tempted to compromise on quality to reduce costs. This would raise profits in the short run because it allows the firm to have high demand (based on its prior reputation) *and* low costs (based on its current actions). But once consumers discover that the seller has been "cheating" by providing a low quality product at a high-quality price, they will normally retaliate by boycotting that supplier in the future. A patient firm will recognize that the short-run surge in profits is usually inadequate to offset the long-run decline.

Can a firm license its reputation? Sometimes. This may be difficult, however, since the licensee will usually make a large gain from abusing the reputation but will not pay a very high share of the consequences of destroying the reputation. This is because the licensee does not internalize the costs to the global reputation of the firm (and therefore all the other licensees) when he engages in localized cheating. Consequently, the reputation-holder (licensor) should use a contract that specifies much more than price. The contract needs to ensure that the licensee provide a level of quality sufficient to maintain the reputation of the licensor. The usual method to achieve such a result in the service industry is a franchise contract, in which the franchisee agrees to an entire business concept.[3] Moreover the franchiser usually engages in extensive monitoring. In some cases, such as accounting, franchise agreements are probably not sufficient to solve the reputation problem. In cases where the upholding of quality requires efforts that are non-verifiable, it may be necessary to keep all overseas producers under common ownership since this will allow for more effective incentive and control systems.

---

[3] The McDonalds 758 page operating manual has rules that specify the exact number of hamburger patties per pound of beef and the amount of sanitizer needed to clean the milk shake machine. For more information, see the webpage of this company specializing in designing operating manuals: `http://www.seniormanagementservices.com/pvt-55F-operation-manuals.htm`.

8.4 Contracts Versus Internalization

Contracts may be problematic under three conditions.

Enforcement: when there is no way to penalize firms who are in breach
of contract.

Verifiability: This is a technical term for situations where courts are
unable to determine whether a breach has even occurred. For instance, suppose the contract calls for a distributor to make "every
effort to find new customers" for the manufacturer. How can a court
of law ever assess whether "every effort" has been made or not?

Unforeseen contingencies: Contracts work best when they spell out exactly what happens in any foreseeable scenario. However, in a world
where the business environment changes in rapid and unpredictable
ways, specifying everything in advance may be impossible. For example, suppose there has been a sharp appreciation of the yen. This
was unanticipated and not included as a clause in the hypothetical
contract with the supplier. Now Toyota really must have the 10%
parts price cut or it will experience a dramatic loss in sales. If the
contract specified a fixed price, there is no flexibility to respond to
unpredicted circumstances.

Consider each of the above problems with contracts. It seems likely
that they will be more important in international business than purely
domestic business. It is hard to use a foreign legal system that is unfamiliar and quite possibly biased to enforce contracts. Furthermore any
ambiguity will be magnified since terms like "every effort" may have
very different connotations in different countries. Finally, there is probably more uncertainty in international business, especially for a firm
that is new to it and does not know what to expect.

With all these arguments against contracting, one might conclude
that it should be used rarely, if ever, in international business transactions. This conclusion would be wrong. Nike does not own its shoe
makers in Asia. Many service companies in the hotel, fast-food, and
retail industries use franchise contracts rather than outright ownership
to expand domestically and internationally. Other examples of contractual rather than ownership-based relationships include the following.

Labatt and Anheuser-Busch established the first Canada-US licensing
relationship in 1980 and recently agreed to extend their relationship
in perpetuity. Labatt brews and markets the Budweiser brand in
Canada. Budweiser is the third largest selling beer in Canada and

outsells all other Canadian-brewed U.S. beer brands combined. A-B's Busch and Michelob brands are imported and distributed by Labatt.

IKEA has a network of 2700 furniture subcontractors located in 67 countries. In some cases IKEA is the exclusive seller of the contractor's furniture and it normally commits to purchase substantial amounts of their output. These firms receive product designs, leased equipment, and technical assistance from IKEA, which designates each product it sells with "Design and Quality, IKEA of Sweden." Despite their aggressively promoted Swedish identity, IKEA group's headquarters is in the Netherlands.

Benetton also relies in large part on independent firms with whom it enters into contractual relationships. Over 95% of total activity (manufacturing and sales) is sub-contracted to outside firms. Suppliers consist of 350 to 400 small, mostly Italian firms. On the sales side, Benetton uses 80 independent agents to manage over 4,000 independently owned stores. Benetton itself carries out some raw material purchases as well as relatively technology-intensive processes such as dyeing and cutting.

These examples show it is possible to conduct upstream (outsourcing) and downstream (wholesale/retail) activities through independent firms even when the firms are located in different countries and when strategic coordination is important. However, there are cases where external relationships tend to break down due to incentive problems. Indeed, internalization has its own costs which must be balanced against the costs of contracting.

Financing costs: It may be that a firm finds it impossible to obtain the funds to buy or establish its own upstream suppliers or downstream distributors. Usually, however, a large multinational based in a developed economy will be better able to finance operations than a small independent firm. Hence, financing costs are probably not the foremost reason for outsourcing.

Value of flexibility: Nike's case shows how a company may benefit from sourcing from multiple suppliers. It has international flexibility to raise and lower orders depending on the evolution of wages and exchange rates. It also has intra-national flexibility to choose the lowest cost supplier and jettison the poor performers. These flexibility benefits are sometimes referred to in discussions of outsourcing as the "variable cost model." The idea is that when you own an operation, the workers are your employees and they become *fixed* costs.

When you outsource to another company, then you have greater freedom in the short run to choose the level of input. The independent supplier will presumably have multiple clients that it can use to diversify the risk from reductions in demand by any one client.

Firm-level comparative advantage: There appears to be a benefit from focusing the top management on a narrow range of tasks. As the span of activities managed by a single firm increases, there will be costs associated with the inability to extend attention across too many tasks. The top managers of a firm are likely to have developed a set of skills in some areas in contrast to their lack of expertise in other areas. The set of things a firm is best at doing are sometimes called "core competencies." Extending the firm to incorporate other businesses where it lacks competence is often a bad idea.

When firm-level comparative advantage is important, a single management team should not take charge of too many tasks and it should concentrate on the tasks where it has a comparative advantage compared to other management teams. The difference between comparative advantage in international trade and the idea we are developing here is that firm-level comparative advantage refers to management teams rather than countries. Consider the following quote from a *McKinsey Quarterly* article on outsourcing:

> "Each skill set requires intensity and management dedication that cannot tolerate dilution. It is hard to imagine Microsofts top managers taking their enthusiasm and skills in software into, say, chip design or even large-scale training in software usage. And if they did, what would be the cost of their loss of attention on software development?" (Quinn and Hilmer, 1995)

Another issue is transferral of risk. One firm may be better able to avoid or bear risks. In particular, foreign firms may worry about expropriation by a host government. If a domestic owner would not face the same risk, then it might make sense for the asset to be sold to him and then controlled by the MNE via contracts. Moving risk to another party via outsourcing does not always make sense. Consider another quote from the same article:

> Gallo, the largest producer and distributor of wines in the United States, outsources most of its grapes, pushing the risks of weather, land prices, and labor problems onto its suppliers. (Quinn and Hilmer, 1995)

This motivation, if true, does not make much sense to me. Consider two cases. First suppose the same weather systems (droughts, for instance) affect all grape farms. Then when weather is bad, the price of grapes will rise and Gallo still bears the risk even if it does not own the vineyards. Second, suppose that weather is highly localized and can be thought of as an idiosyncratic shock hurting one farm at the same time as another farm flourishes. Then the vineyard owners who receive bad weather cannot simply raise prices. They will however probably need to purchase some form of crop insurance. With free-entry in the vineyard business driving prices towards average costs, the insurance costs will tend to be passed on to Gallo. If Gallo had owned all the vineyards, it would have possessed some built-in self-insurance against localized bad weather. My guess about Gallo's outsourcing decision is that it derives from the goal of focusing top management's attention on their comparative advantages in making and marketing wine, activities that probably involve quite different skill sets from grape-growing.

8.5 Internal Allocation of Resources

One of the key roles of headquarters in most multi-divisional firms is to allocate funding for new investment across divisions. Does it make sense to "internalize" the financing of investment in this way or would firms be better off writing debt or equity contracts directly with external financiers (banks etc.)? A second key role is the assignment of key personnel to run particular subsidiaries. The *Economist* magazine recently reconsidered "Conglomerates in developing countries." When countries like the U.S. embrace "dis-integration" of large firms into individual focused firms, the economies of less developed countries are dominated by large conglomerates. Do these firms, such as Korea's *chaebol* retard development? The article points out that they may simply reflect a country's lack of development of "specialized intermediaries."

> In the market for capital, these [intermediaries] are mutual funds, venture capitalists, equity analysts, auditors, and so forth. In the market for labour, they include executive-search firms, vocational and business schools, and certification agencies. In the markets for products and ideas, they include intellectual property lawyers and consumer activists... [Poor countries today have few such intermediaries.]
> Hence the appeal of conglomerates. They are their own intermediaries. In a country that lacks a functioning stock market, a conglomerate can channel cash from one business to another. If education levels are low, it picks the brightest, trains them

in one subsidiary and transfers them to another. If property, contract and liability laws are confusing and the courts are venal, it substitutes the group's reputation in transactions. (*The Economist* January 5th, 2002, p. 59)

The article goes on to acknowledge that these activities all have potential dark sides. Internal capital markets can be criticized as "cross-subsidization" or "empire-building." The former occurs when a firm channels cash from a profitable subsidiary into low-return investments in a poorly performing subsidiary. The latter occurs when the manager expands the firm for his own egotistical pleasure. Internal labour markets can fall into "cronyism" or nepotism. We see the same good and bad possibilities as inherent to the multinational enterprise which can be seen as a kind of "border-straddling" conglomerate. The difference is that the multinational not only replaces intermediaries within a particular host country, it also replaces intermediaries that are often lacking for facilitating movement of capital and labour between countries. Essentially the top management's role is to identify funds and personnel that are under-utilized in the country where they currently reside and transfer them to another country with great opportunities but insufficient resources.

While the funds for investment are essentially homogeneous, the talented personnel are not. The key issue is to devise a means of identifying raw talent and then augmenting it. An important use of subsidiaries is as a laboratory to assess skills. Promising managers can be placed in charge of small subsidiaries which are used as testing grounds. There may also be valuable learning-by-doing that can later be transferred (with the promoted manager) to more important subsidiaries.

One argument in favour of internal finance is that the headquarters (HQ) of a corporation has better information about the quality of investment opportunities than would an outsider such as a bank. This asymmetry creates a role for HQ to "rob from the rich and give to the poor"—move cash from divisions with lots of funds but few profitable investment opportunities to divisions in the opposite situation. Thus a conglomerate like USX could use cash generated by its oil refining business to finance new investments in its steel division during periods where oil prices were high. Similarly a firm with investments in the Netherlands and Namibia might move cash from the former to the latter as it takes advantage of its well-developed position in the Netherlands to fund new development in Namibia.

Table 8.1 illustrates how the Robin Hood strategy might be employed. The matrix resembles a framework introduced by the Boston

Table 8.1. MNE as Robin Hood

		Resources(Capital and Talent)	
		Insufficient	Adequate
Business Opportunity	Bad	a ("Bum")	b ("Angel")
	Good	c ("Entrepreneur")	d ("Lone Ranger")

Consulting Group (BCG) some time ago. It should be noted, however that the column and row categories of the BCG matrix contain somewhat different concepts. They use market share (instead of resources) for the columns and industry growth (instead of opportunities) for the rows. This means that the BCG matrix is not really appropriate for consideration of resource allocation within the firm.

Under the Robin Hood strategy, the MNE would move funds from countries in cell b (so-called "angels"), with lots of money but no good opportunities for investment, to cell c, the "entrepreneur," which is in the opposite position. It will want to shut down or sell off subsidiaries in cell a (the "bums") and subsidiaries in cell d (the "lone rangers") are basically self-financing.

The Robin-Hood strategy might be seen as a form of "corporate socialism," since it seems to operate according to the principle of "from each according to his ability, to each according to his needs."[4] Not surprisingly, then, there is some evidence that it does not work very well in practice. The main problem lies with the assumption that HQ is well-informed regarding the investment opportunities of divisions. It is more likely to be the case that the divisions actively attempt to influence HQ to channel funds their way. In terms of the table, HQ may not be able to distinguish between subsidiaries in cells a and c. Both will claim to be in cell c. Similarly, amongst high cash flow subsidiaries, all will claim to be in cell d, i.e. that they can put all their funds to good use.

Many actions (lobbying, under-reporting cash-flow, presenting overly optimistic forecasts) can seriously distort the allocation of funds. The worst-case scenario is a flow of funds from firms in cell d to cell a. When

---

[4] The direction of redistribution need not be unidirectional. Since business cycles are not highly correlated across nations, the MNE could raise funds in countries at the tail-end of a "boom" and invest in countries just emerging from recessions.

many large conglomerates were dismantled and the parts sold off during the 1980s it was generally found that the value of the individual parts exceeded the value of the whole. Thus the activities of HQ in diversified conglomerates appears to be *value-destroying*. I am not aware of any studies of this kind focusing on the break-up of MNEs. However, I have heard of cases where the Canadian divisions of US owned firms devoted considerable resources to convincing headquarters to allocate funds for them to invest in various projects. The managers of the divisions may have an incentive to over-invest since they may capture benefits from managing large amounts of assets without having to bear the true costs of the investments.

The model of MNEs using their HQ to collect and redistribute cash-flow *à la* Robin Hood does not appear to be very attractive. There may however be another role for the MNE in conducting internal finance that makes more sense.

Consider the role of venture capitalists. They provide start-up money for new firms, usually in high technology fields. They differ from traditional banks in their willingness to gamble on firms without much of a proven track record. They also differ in the services they provide the client. Unlike a bank, a primary role of the venture capitalist is to contribute expertise in evaluating and developing the idea of the entrepreneur.[5]

A new overseas production facility is, in many respects, like a new firm in a high technology industry. Both have high upfront costs that must be born before a profit can be expected. Both have great uncertainty on the eventual size of the market since consumers may reject the new product. Finally, there are questions regarding productions costs. The headquarters of the MNE possesses specialized knowledge over its product range and the production process. It is in a much better position than outside financiers to decide whether a new overseas venture will pay off. Moreover, it may transfer the expertise gained in prior investments to the investment in a new country. Thus one model of the expanding MNE is one in which HQ is an intermediary between financiers who are willing to take a risk, but who have little specialized information, and the new subsidiaries that require funds. In this model, as more information about the prospects of the subsidiary becomes publicly available, the MNE should restructure its finances to make greater use of external capital markets which are less subject to political influence than the internal market.

---

[5] Sometimes they will often go as far as to replace the founder with a professional manager.

References

Quinn, James Brian and Frederick G Hilmer, 1995, "Make versus buy: Strategic outsourcing," *The McKinsey Quarterly* No. 1, pp. 48–70. Online access at http://www.mckinseyquarterly.com.

Holmstrom, B. and J. Roberts, 1998, "The Boundaries of the Firm Revisited," *Journal of Economics Perspectives* Vol. 12, No. 4.

Bolton, P. and D. Scharfstein, 1998, "Corporate Finance, the Theory of the Firm, and Organizations" *Journal of Economics Perspectives* Vol. 12, No. 4.

United Nations, 1995, *World Investment Report.*

Williamson, Oliver, 1975, *Markets and Hierarchies: Analysis and Antitrust Implications.* New York: Free Press.

9

Competitive Interactions

Chapter 7 focused on a set of issues that affect all firms that are trying to construct a locational strategy that spans international borders. We argued that firms should select from amongst many possible international production strategies the one that best resolves the tradeoffs between the four elements: factor advantages, trade costs, market sizes, and scale economies. My view is that the four elements should be the most important influences on where to deploy a firm's resources. If building a factor in, say, Vietnam, makes no sense based on the four elements, then it probably is a bad idea. Nevertheless, there is another consideration that many managers invoke to justify the location and timing of their outward investments: the actions of rival firms. In this chapter we will consider how interactions with competitors affect location strategy of the multinational. We will examine some simple situations in which the location and timing of investment decisions depend critically on the actions of a firm's competitors.

9.1 Motivating Examples

To set the stage for the analysis that follows, we will briefly review a few episodes that may illustrate competitive interactions in practice.

9.1.1 SUVs in the USA

In 1990 both BMW and Mercedes served the world's largest auto market using their factories in Germany. During the 1990s this changed, with both firms establishing factories in states in the Southeast of the US. The following time-line shows when the factories were established and also how BMW altered its production plans. The time-line also shows later investments by Hyundai and Nissan in the same region of the US.

1992 BMW picks Greer, South Carolina, as the site for a car production plant.

1993 Mercedes announces it will build sport utility vehicles (SUVs) in new factory in Vance, Alabama.

1994 BMW plant begins production of the 318i at Greer.

1995 BMW plants starts to produce Z3 roadster at Greer.

1997 Mercedes begins M-class production at Vance.

1998 BMW decides to expand the Greer plant and use it to produce the X5 (a new SUV).

2002 Hyundai announces plant in Montgomery, Alabama. Production to begin in 2005.

2003 Nissan begins car production in Canton, Mississippi in May.

2003 Mercedes announces $600 million expansion of the Vance plant, with 2000 employees to be added by early 2005.

Mercedes seemed to follow its rival BMW in producing vehicles in the Southeast of the US. However, BMW followed Mercedes in producing an SUV there (although BMW called the X5 a "sports *activity* vehicle").

9.1.2 Retail in China

With the world's largest population and decades of rapid growth in per capita income, China has become one of the largest retail markets in the world. Now Wal-Mart (the world's largest retailer, based in the US), Carrefour (the second largest, based in France), and Metro (the third, based in Germany) have all entered China. The timing and location of their entries are highly suggestive.

Carrefour was the first to arrive, setting up its first "hyper-store" in the nation's capital, Beijing, in 1995. The following year Wal-Mart established its first super-center in Shenzhen, a rapidly growing export-oriented city near Hong Kong. Also in 1996, Metro opened its first store in Shanghai. Since then all three firms expanded considerably. As of early 2006, the first mover, Carrefour had the largest presence, with 70 hypermarkets and 225 discount stores. Wal-mart had 56 stores but later in 2006 announced plans to expand via an acquisition. Metro was the smallest, with 30 discount (cash-only) outlets.

KFC and McDonalds established their networks of franchise restaurants around the same time. KFC moved first and established a restaurant in Beijing in 1987. McDonalds moved three years later and opened its first restaurant in Shenzhen. The company did not cede Beijing to KFC and instead established its largest restaurant in the world there in 1992. By 2006 there were 680 McDonalds restaurants in China, considerably less than the over 1400 KFCs.[1]

9.2 Key Concepts

Analyzing the situations where actor's payoffs are interdependent requires the use of some game theory. There are two key concepts that need to be introduced right away: *strategic complementarity* and *first-mover advantages.*

Strategic complementarity means that if you do more of something, then the payoff to me of doing that thing increases. The alternative is strategic substitutability. In that case you doing something makes that thing *less* attractive to me. To take an example from outside of location strategy, consider the purchase of advertising time during the Superbowl. If Pepsi's decision to advertise during the game makes it more attractive for Coca Cola to advertise then (and vice-versa), we say the firm's advertising decisions are strategic complements. Location decisions would be strategic complements for Japanese auto-makers if Honda's decision to manufacture in some state or country made that place more attractive to Toyota.

First-mover advantages (FMA) is a notion that is invoked frequently, but rarely defined unambiguously. The basic idea is that the first one to do something, obtains a lasting advantage over subsequent imitators. The "something" in question is often the introduction of a new product. Thus one could debate whether the Apple Ipod's strong market share (as of 2006) and ample profit margins derive from being the first mover in the digital audio player market. This is a topic for general strategy books. Our interest here is in the location aspect of the FMA. Does the first firm to establish operations in China retain a sustained advantage over subsequent entrants? If so, we say there is an FMA.

Strategic complementarity is important for deciding whether to invest in a region or not. The presence of first-mover advantages determines the optimal *timing* of entry into region. In the next two subsections we explore the underlying forces that lead to strategic comple-

---

[1] The information on the entry of Carrefour, Wal-mart, KFC and McDonalds into China was collected by Ran Jing from the Chinese language websites of each corporation. Roberts (2005) provides a good overview of the recent "retail wars" in China.

mentarity and first-mover advantages. This is important if one is to be able to apply the concepts in practice.

9.2.1 Sources of Strategic Complementarity

There are very different mechanisms behind strategic complementarity in MNE location decisions that have been considered by economists and management professors.

- Agglomeration economies or Cluster advantages: Marshall (1920) and Porter (1990) described how groups of related firms often perform better (higher productivity, more competitive products) when they choose geographically proximate locations.
- Informational herding: Choices made by others may reveal information they gathered on the attractiveness of a location.
- Oligopolistic reaction: Knickerbocker (1973) argued that in industries with a small number of firms, the follower matches the leader's move to maintain competitive stability.

The most well-documented cause of strategic complementarities are mainly referred to by economists as *agglomeration economies*. They are similar in some respect to plant-level scale economies except that they occur at the level of a region, rather than a factory. The idea is that the greater the scale of an activity at a regional level, the lower will be the average costs of undertaking that activity.

Marshall (1920) described the three classic causes of agglomerations economies. The first is what we now call "knowledge spillovers." In an often-quoted passage, Marshall wrote that when people in the same line of business locate near each other,

> "The mysteries of the trade become no mysteries; but are as it were in the air, and children learn many of them unconsciously. Good work is rightly appreciated, inventions and improvements in machinery, in processes and the general organization of the business have their merits promptly discussed: if one man starts a new idea, it is taken up by others and combined with suggestions of their own; and thus it becomes the source of further new ideas."

While his language style seems dated, his ideas seem so current that one almost thinks he must have been talking about Silicon Valley.

The second point has to do with what Marshall called "subsidiary" industries and Porter calls "related and supporting" industries. Marshall's idea was that the bigger is the local cluster in the downstream

industry, the more suppliers will be willing to sink capital into specialized machinery. Porter tells a similar story: a cluster of downstream
rivals will stimulate the formation of a cluster of proximate upstream
suppliers. These firms will create advantages for the downstream firms
because they "deliver the most cost-effective inputs in an efficient, early,
rapid, and sometimes preferential way."

Finally, Marshall argued that groups of firms attract skilled workers
and vice-versa.

> "The owner of an isolated factory, even if he has access to a
> plentiful supply of general labour, is often put to great shifts
> for want of some special skilled labour; and a skilled workman,
> when thrown out of employment in it, has no easy refuge."

Porter (1990) argues that on top of these benefits, by locating near
your strongest rivals, you set into motion forces that will ultimately
make your firm more competitive. The presence of local rivals creates
"pressure on companies to innovate and improve." The rivals vie for the
"bragging rights" of being the best in the cluster and they can offer "no
excuses" for relatively poor performance. In the short run, then, local
rivalry makes life rather unpleasant for managers. But Porter assures
us that in the long run, "dynamic improvement" will create sustainable
competitive advantages.

The Marshall and Porter analysis of industry clusters has implications for multinational firms. When other MNCs in the same industry
establish operations in a country, then this will create cluster advantages for the remaining firms in the industry. For example, Ireland has
established a strong cluster in the information communications technology (ICT) sector. The Irish Development Agency (IDA) reports that in
2006 there were 109,000 employees in the sector of which 45,000 worked
for foreign firms such as IBM, Intel, Dell, Apple, Hewlett-Packard, and
Microsoft. There are 1300 firms in all and seven out of the ten largest
MNCs in the ICT sector have a "substantial base" there. The large
number of suppliers and the IDA's claim that Ireland has the highest proportion of science graduates in Europe both support the Mar-
shall/Porter arguments for clusters based on specialized inputs and
highly skilled workers.

Informational herding leads to a very different type of strategic complementarity. The best example is only loosely related to international
business but it is something that most travellers experience repeatedly.
After checking into a hotel in an unfamiliar city, you set out to find
a restaurant for dinner. Someone suggests a restaurant that looks fine
and has affordable prices. But you decide not to enter because there

is no one else inside. If your reluctance to eat there is simply because you like the noise and bustle of a crowded restaurant, then this would just be another application of the agglomeration economies described above. However, suppose you actually prefer a quiet and uncrowded restaurant. You might nevertheless avoid this restaurant because you fear that the lack of customers is a sign of poor quality. Then you would continue to search until you found a place that was sufficiently full so as to inspire confidence in the quality.

Multinational location decisions have some of the same features as choosing a restaurant in a new city. The MNE is often uncertain about a variety of things. Is there a good market for the product we make? How productive are the workers? Is the infrastructure reliable? Are the politicians, bureaucrats, and courts corrupt? One can learn some general features from publicly available data but it is often very difficult to infer the attractiveness of a location for a specific industry. After conducting some initial research, the MNE formulates a guess—but it is just one guess. Alternatively, one can rely more on the information gathered by other firms. If all the firms in an industry have chosen Ireland as their base for serving the European market, that may be seen as a persuasive vote of confidence. Even without direct (Marshall/Porter) cluster advantages, the MNE might decide to locate in the cluster because of the collective wisdom embodied in the other firms' decisions.

The third type of complementarity, *oligopolistic reaction*, is also related to uncertainty about production and market conditions in a foreign country. Knickerbocker (1973) studied data on US multinational's overseas investments and concluded that the tendency of firms to invest in the same countries at approximately the same time was strongest in oligopolies (industries with a just a few firms). His story emphasized the damage that one firm could suffer if its rival was the sole producer in a country that turned out to be a great production location. Knickerbocker's basic thesis is best described in the following quote explaining how a firm lowers risk by following a rival into a foreign market:

"To illustrate, if firm B [the follower] matched, move for move, the acts of its rival, firm A [the leader], B would have roughly the same chance as A to exploit each foreign market opportunity. Thus for each new market penetrated by both A and B, B's gains, either in terms of earnings or in terms of the acquisition of new capabilities, would parallel those of A. If some of A's moves turned out to be failures, B's losses would be in the range of those of A. Neither firm would be better or worse off. From the point of view of firm B, this matching strategy guaranteed

that its competitive capabilities would be roughly in balance
with those of firm A." (page 24–25)

Knickerbocker never wrote down a mathematical version of his ideas so
we can only speculate on what exactly he was assuming. Reading the
story now, it appears to have been influenced by the Cold War notions
of "balance of power" between the USA and the USSR.

One way to think about oligopolistic reaction is that it is a story
in which managers care only about relative performance and are seeking to minimize the probability of being the under-performer. This
might seem superficially appealing until one realizes that a firm that
consistently engages in oligopolistic reaction will pass up opportunities
to earn higher expected profits by taking a different course from that
taken by rivals. As a result, the strategy of matching a rival's moves is
not likely to yield high returns for shareholders.

Thierry Mayer, John Ries and I wrote a paper where we reinter-
preted Knickerbocker's hypothesis using a standard model of oligopoly.
We found that firms usually do better by choosing *different* production
locations: what we called *reverse oligopolistic reaction*. The reason for
avoiding each other is something called the *market crowding effect*.
The basic idea is that when a company faces a nearby competitor, it
is forced to charge lower prices and cede a larger portion of the market than when its competitor reaches the market via exports from a
remote production site. The reason is that trade costs insulate a firm
from vigourous competition from a distant rival. This makes it desirable
to put some "space" between us.

The market crowding effect is stronger for goods that are undif-
ferentiated and therefore close substitutes for each other. For example
consider a highway exit where there is currently only one gas station.
If a second one opens at the same exit, they will have to share the
market. They will probably compete harder for the same customers,
pushing down the price. At the national level, consider a country like
Brazil that had high tariffs on imported autos. The first foreign maker
to producer there (Volkswagen) had something of a captive market.
The second firm will tend to "crowd" the market, lowering the price
and per-firm volume.

Choosing distinct locations can also help to mitigate crowding effects in factor markets. If my competitor is seeking the same key managers or production sites as me, we will bid up salaries and land prices.
Unless, there is a vigorous supply response that more than offsets the
demand increase—possible in the case of skilled managers (according

to Marshall) but not conceivable for land—firms would be better off leaving each other alone.

If market crowding effects are strong relative to agglomeration effects, then firms' location decisions can be *strategic substitutes* instead of strategic complements. Since clusters and imitative FDI decisions seem much more common than firms that choose isolated locations, we may be inclined to think that location decisions are never strategic substitutes. That is probably a mistake. One cause of the mistake is a thing called "common cause."

Why do we see clusters of gas stations near highway exits, wineries in the Southern Okanagan valley, offshore financing corporations on Caribbean islands? One reason is that in each of these cases there is a local attraction that appeals to all potential entrants. In the case of gas stations, it is the cars emerging from the exit ramp in need of gas. For the wineries, it is the sunny and relatively warm climate, combined with the night-time cooling effect of the lake. For the offshore financing companies it is the low taxes and lenient financial reporting requirements offered by the tax haven governments (see Chapter 12). The existence of a *common cause* driving location decisions can mask the existence of strategic substitution in a case like the gas stations. It can also give the appearance of strong strategic complementarity even when those effects are weak or absent.

Consider the following case. The dean of XXXX School of Business announces a new MBA to be offered in Shanghai, China. When confronted with skepticism, he announces that other big-name US business schools have launched MBA programs in China and "we need to get on the boat." The question is whether the presence of other MBA programs raises the payoff to XXXX of establishing its own program. The fact that other MBAs have chosen to set up programs in Shanghai may reflect common cause. The growth of outward-oriented business in Shanghai has created a pool of managers seeking advanced business education programs that existing universities in China do not know how to offer. However, since XXXX and its US rivals will compete for the same pool of students and even some of the same skilled lecturers, market-crowding effects may be strong enough to imply a strategic substitutes setting. The XXXX School might be better off avoiding Shanghai and establishing in another city with similar demand conditions that is not yet served by other programs.

9.2.2 Sources of First-Mover Advantages

We now turn to the second key concept: when is there an advantage due to moving *first*? And if you do not get to move first for one reason or another is it better to be the *last* mover or should one try to move as *early* as possible?

There are two main sources of first-mover advantages.

- scarce *resource preemption*: In a "first-come, first-serve" situation, the early firm seizes the most prized resource and later movers have to settle for less attractive alternatives.
- consumer *switching costs*: the amount a customer who has been buying from a given seller must give up (in time, money, or expected benefit) in order to switch to a different seller's product.

Resources subject to preemption include uniquely advantaged retail sites and production sites. Sometimes foreign investors seek to obtain a whole set of such resources by acquiring an existing domestic firm that has managed to assemble an attractive resource portfolio. The second best acquisition target may possess a substantially inferior set of assets. Similarly, in countries where the preferred mode of entry is a joint venture, there will often be potential partners that are much more attractive than others.

In a well-functioning market economy, the resource preemption effect may not confer much of an advantage to the first-mover. The reason is that the market will tend to price resources according to their values. Hence, the most attractive acquisition target is also likely to be sold at the highest price, lowering the net gains of moving first. Even a non-market asset, such as a site permit for building a factory, may be available only at high "price"—in the form of offers the firm must make to government officials.

The form and magnitude of switching costs depends on the nature of the good. One distinction is between search and experience goods. In the case of the former, attributes of the goods are known before the first purchase—all that is required is a search to find the product. If a new firm enters a market, consumers may be willing to switch easily as long as they are aware of the new entrant's product and therefore do not need to search for it. For experience goods, the consumer learns the quality of the product after buying it and trying it and sometimes the evaluation period is protracted (e.g. cars). Experience goods are likely to engender greater consumer loyalty because once the buyer has identified a product that works, she may be reluctant to take the risk of trying one that will not work. A third type of good requires the consumer to invest time in learning how to operate it. Examples include software, video games, and some types of machine tools. This learning is an irreversible investment and it will take a large inducement in terms of superior quality or price to persuade some customers to repeat their investment in a new product.

When switching costs are large the firm that enters first in effect takes "ownership" of a large set of customers. These customers can be wooed away by new entrants but only at the cost of selling at a low (or even negative) profit margin for an extended period. This leads to first-mover advantages, which extend to a lesser degree to other early movers. The worst situation is to be a late mover.

There is a powerful force offsetting first-mover advantages: the investments of early movers generate spillover benefits for followers. For example, a firm that introduces a new product to a country often has to teach consumers about the desirability and uses of the product. When subsequent firms enter with competing products, they find an educated consumer base already in place. The sort of educational process operates for workers and managers. The first mover trains potential employees for the followers. Furthermore, legal issues involving production permits and government product approval can be resolved at great cost by the pioneering firm. Followers may find a well-functioning legal framework already in place. One of the most important spillovers is probably knowledge about which business practices work well in a new business environment. If followers pay close attention to the leader's experience, they will be able to copy effective strategies and avoid failed approaches.

In the history of new products, *an early mover rather than the first mover, usually ends up on top.* The Apple iPod was not the first digital audio player (it had been introduced three years earlier by a Korean manufacturer named SaeHan). Google was not the first internet search engine. Excel and Word were not the first spreadsheet or word processor programs. But all three entered fairly early in the life cycle of these products and now it would be very hard for a new entrant to dislodge them as the dominant players.

The history of country investments by multinationals provides mixed evidence for first-mover advantages. The two first foreign companies to manufacture in China were Volkswagen (1984, Shanghai) and Peugeot (1985, Guangzhou). Fourteen years later, many other firms had entered but Volkswagen was the dominant player, taking 50% of the market.[2] On the other hand Peugeot had bailed out, selling its factory to Honda.

---

[2] *New York Times*, December 18, 1998.

Another early entrant, Jeep (part of AMC at the time, but later part of Chrysler), also failed to succeed in China. On the other hand, GM entered China relatively late, producing its first car there in 1999. Nevertheless China became a profitable market for GM and its market share there moved ahead of VW in 2005 (11% versus 9%). This is of course just one case and the Chinese auto market is very dynamic, with late entrant Toyota expected to see its current market share of about 3.5% increase substantially as a result of recent investments.[3] The point of this case is to illustrate that while we cannot dismiss the importance of first-mover advantages, we should not exaggerate them either.

9.3 Multinational Location Games

We now use some simple game theory to explore how the concepts from the previous section influence competitive interactions. To make things concrete, let us consider the case of Mercedes and BMW trying to decide where to place factories to assemble their new Sport Utility Vehicles (SUVs). We will assume throughout this example that plant-level economies of scale are so important that each firm will only have a single factory. The German location has the advantage of placing the SUV factory close to parts suppliers and their main design engineers. The SUV line might even be added within an existing factory. Despite their high wages, German workers might offer factor advantages based on their high skill in making luxury cars. Offsetting these considerations is the savings in downstream trade costs achievable by locating production within the major market for high-end SUVs: the USA. There are lower transport costs, better feedback from customers, and avoiding possible tariffs on luxury vehicles that might emerge in a future trade conflict. Thus, the basic attractiveness of Germany and the USA depend in large part on the elements of multinational strategy that we brought together in Chapter 7. Each of these elements applies even if the rival company were not planning to produce an SUV at all.

How then do the BMW and Mercedes decisions relate to each other? First consider the payoffs in Table 9.1.

It is not difficult to see that these payoffs strongly argue for the two companies to make different decisions. To see this, we should look for the Nash Equilibria. A Nash Equilibria is an outcome of the game that neither side would want to deviate unilaterally from. This game

---

[3] *Associated Press Online*, May 19, 2006

Table 9.1. Location choices for Mercedes and BMW SUV factories: the symmetric case

		Mercedes chooses	
		USA	Germany
BMW chooses	USA	1, 1	**2**, 2
	Germany	2, **2**	**1**, 1

has two Nash Equilibria: (BMW in USA, Mercedes in Germany) and (BMW in Germany, Mercedes in USA) In both situations, only one firm produce in the US while the other make its SUV in Germany. Underlying these payoffs are market-crowding effects. If Mercedes is the only firm in the USA it can sell more SUVs at higher prices than if it faces *local* competition from BMW. Thus, strategic substitution implies that following your rival makes no sense. If Mercedes chooses to produce in the USA, BMW will be better off producing in Germany and concentrating on sales to the European market.

The payoffs in Table 9.1 were chosen to neutralize the effects of factor advantages and market sizes that would normally bias the location decision in favour of one country or the other. This situation artificially made each firm indifferent as to the two countries for any reason other than the rival's decision.

Suppose instead that the USA market is much larger and its factor costs are quite competitive as well. Then both firms would rather jointly locate in the USA than jointly locate in Germany. Table 9.2 provides some numbers in which the USA is intrinsically preferred. This case also features very large market-crowding effects. One way to see this is to sum the profits of the two firms. The two firms could earn a total of 7 by choosing different countries. However, if they matched location choices, combined profits could be as low as $1 + 1 = 2$ if they chose Germany.

What is the equilibrium of this game? If the firms chose locations simultaneously, BMW in the USA and Mercedes in Germany is a Nash Equilibrium but so is Mercedes in the USA and BMW in Germany. If one firm could move first, it would select the USA. The rational response of the rival would be to choose Germany. This would give it more profits than co-locating in the USA (3 vs 2) but less profit than the first mover (3 vs 4). Thus we have a case with a first-mover advantage caused by a combination of location differences and market-crowding. Even though the USA is considered the better location, and it is the place the first mover selects, it is unwise, given these payoffs for the other firm to follow it.

Table 9.2. Location choices for Mercedes and BMW SUV factories: when the USA is a "better" location.

| | | Mercedes chooses | |
		USA	Germany
	USA	**2**, 2	**4**, 3
BMW chooses			
	Germany	**3**, 4	**1**, 1

The payoffs in Table 9.2 do not help us to understand what actually happened since they predict that only one of the two firms would have selected the USA. There are two distinct ways to alter the payoffs to yield a game that predicts both firms choosing the USA.

First, we could strengthen the inherent advantage of the USA. To see this, increase the payoffs of choosing the US by two, regardless of what the other firm is doing. As shown in Table 9.3, the market-crowding effects (which would remain since each firm would still improve its profit if the other firm chose a different country) are no longer strong enough to separate the firms. Regardless of what the other firm chooses, each firm prefers the US location.[4] Since the follower's location can not be influenced, being the first mover is of no value. Both firms obtain a payoff of 4 in either case. What *would* be useful is for the firms to get together and agree to choose different locations. Then they could achieve a combined profit of 9 instead of 8. However, this outcome would require the firm in the USA to compensate the firm in Germany, a transaction that might be difficult to execute in practice.

Table 9.4 illustrates a second, and more interesting, way to explain why both Mercedes and BMW chose to produce their SUVs in the USA. As in the preceding game, we make the US intrinsically more

---

[4] In the terminology of game theory, we would say that the payoffs of this game make one option (the USA) the "dominant strategy."

Table 9.3. Location choices for Mercedes and BMW SUV factories: when the USA is a *much* better location.

		Mercedes chooses	
		USA	Germany
BMW chooses	USA	**4**, 4	**6**, 3
	Germany	3, **6**	1, 1

attractive. The big difference is that the new payoffs exhibit strategic complementarity. We can see this by starting from the position of both firms in Germany. Neither firm would want to *unilaterally* move to the US because its profit would fall from 3 to 2. But if both firms were to choose the USA, their individual and combined profits would be maximized.

Table 9.4. Location choices for Mercedes and BMW SUV factories: agglomeration effects

		Mercedes chooses	
		USA	Germany
BMW chooses	USA	**4**, 4	**2**, 1
	Germany	1, 2	**3**, 3

This new set of pay-offs yields two Nash equilibria for simultaneous location choices: Both can produce in Germany or both can produce in the USA. This set of pay-offs is called a "coordination game." There is no conflict between the interests of the two firms. Indeed, as long as they can communicate their intentions to each other, it is easy to coordinate on the choice that maximizes both firms' profits. What underlies this payoff structure? First of all, market-crowding effects must be small enough that they are overwhelmed by other determinants of payoffs. Market crowding might be weak because the two German companies would be primarily stealing customers from American and Japanese SUV makers rather than from each other. Alternatively, if transport costs are low relative to the value of the product, then the market could be essentially global. This will tend to lead to small market-crowding effects because far-away competitors are just as important as nearby ones.

The payoffs in Table 9.4 do not just exhibit a lack of market-crowding effects; they suggest the presence of agglomeration effects. Why in practice would two auto plants obtain an *advantage* from locating near each other? One important reason is that they will share information about how to produce efficiently in whatever location they choose. Some information would be related to SUV manufacture; other information would be related to the location itself, such as tips for finding qualified workers. More importantly, for the auto industry, the co-location in the same area of the US will encourage parts suppliers to set up in the same area, giving both firms access to cheaper and more reliable sources of components. In summary, *a combination of strong agglomeration economies and weak market crowding effects generates a coordination game in location choice.*

Note that if one firm can choose its location first, this leader would certainly choose the USA and the second-mover would match locations. Note the first mover obtains no advantage—and the second mover no disadvantage—because both firms agree that the USA is their preferred location.

Table 9.5 modifies the situation slightly to create a more complex situation. As in Table 9.4, there are agglomeration effects. This can be seen in that collective profit when the firms choose common location $(4+3=7)$ is higher than when they choose different locations $(2+1=3)$. The key difference between the games in Tables 9.4 and 9.5 is that now Mercedes prefers that they choose Germany (which will give it a pay-off of 4) while BMW prefers the USA.

Games of this form are often called a "battle of the sexes."[5] This game has a first-mover advantage. If BMW could choose first it would choose the USA and Mercedes would (reluctantly) follow. BMW would earn higher profits than Mercedes. BMW's payoff is also higher than it would have been as the second mover (in which case Mercedes would have selected the equilibrium in which both firms stayed in Germany).

---

[5] The original version has a couple named Pat and Chris trying decide whether to go to a boxing match or a ballet on Saturday night. Pat likes boxing but Chris likes ballet but since they like each other, they prefer being together over being alone even if it means going to the less desirable event.

The value of the first mover advantage can be thought of as the amount of money a firm would be willing to pay prior to starting the game to be able to move first when the game began. In this case the value is $4 - 3 = 1$.

The game illustrated in Table 9.5 makes a general point about location choice. With agglomeration effects (causing firms to want to locate together) and asymmetric preferences (one firm's payoffs tend to be higher in a particular location) there is an advantage in being the leader, because the firm that chooses first ends up selecting where both will locate.

Table 9.5. Location choices for Mercedes and BMW SUV factories: agglomeration economies with asymmetric preferences

		Mercedes chooses	
		USA	Germany
BMW chooses	USA	4, 3	**2**, 1
	Germany	1, 2	**3**, 4

In this section we have seen how to build agglomeration effects and market-crowding effects into the payoffs for settings in which two firms are deciding where to produce. We have analyzed five "games" these firms play using the "normal" (tabular) form of the game. This form is useful because it allows us to consider simultaneous moves as well as when one firm or the other has the opportunity to move first. However, most people find it easier to understand the sequential-move games when they are expressed in *extensive* form, i.e. as decision "trees."

Figure 9.1 uses the tree representation for a location game that is designed to capture some aspects of the Carrefour and Wal-mart story from sub-section 9.1.2. The tree is set up such that Carrefour chooses its base first. The upper "branch" corresponds to Beijing and the lower branch is Shenzhen. For simplicity, we imagine the other possible locations are substantially less attractive and can therefore be omitted from the figure. After Carrefour chooses, Wal-mart can copy its location—the upper "twig" coming out of each upper branch—or select the alternative twig. The payoffs are shown at the end of the twigs, with

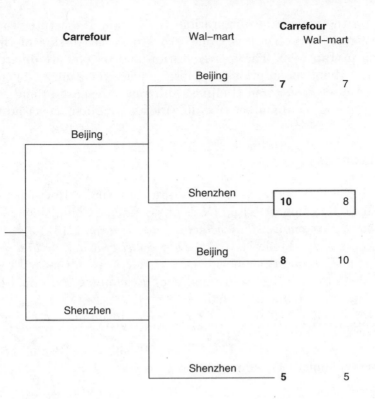

Fig. 9.1. Extensive form of a location game

Carrefour's profit shown in **bold** on the left, and Wal-mart's shown on the right.

If Carrefour is smart, it should figure out Wal-mart's best responses. Inspecting the payoffs on the right, we see that Wal-mart is slightly better off choosing Shenzhen when Carrefour has chosen Beijing and it is much more profitable if Carrefour selects Shenzhen and Wal-mart can have Beijing to itself. The payoffs shown here combine two important features. First, we have a situation of *strategic substitutes*: the second mover wants to avoid the location selected by the first mover. The likely explanation for such payoffs is *market crowding*. Second, there is a basic asymmetry between locations: Beijing is preferable. The aggregate profit when both choose Beijing, 14, is higher than the aggregate profit when both choose Shenzhen, 10. Of course the market crowding effect implies that the firms will not want to choose the same location. Thus, the important thing is that when Carrefour selects Beijing and Wal-mart goes to Shenzhen the profit for Carrefour is higher, 10, than in the opposite configuration, 8. By now the astute reader will have figured out that this game is a sequential version of the game shown in Table 9.2. The representation and payoffs are different, but the underlying assumptions and message are the same. The combination of a better location (Beijing's inherent advantages) and strategic substitutes (due to market crowding) leads to a first-mover advantage.

References

Head, Keith, Thierry Mayer, and John Ries, 2002, "Revisiting Oligopolistic Reaction: Are FDI Decisions Strategic Complements?" *Journal of Economics, Management, and Strategy*, 11(3).

Knickerbocker, Frederic, 1973, *Oligopolistic Reaction and Multinational Enterprise,* Cambridge, MA: Harvard University Press.

Marshall, Alfred, 1920, *Principles of Economics* 8th ed., Book IV, Chapter X, London: MacMillan.

Porter, Michael, 1990, *The Competitive Advantage of Nations* New York: The Free Press.

Roberts, Dexter, 2005, "Let China's Retail Wars Begin," *Business Week* January 17 online edition.

10

Foreign Exchange Risk

In a perfect world exchange rates would not matter. In a world of perfectly tradeable goods and perfectly flexible prices, the relative price—expressed in their respective home currencies—of each good would have to come to rest at the exchange rate. Another way of thinking about it is that the Canadian government could pass a law declaring that henceforward the Canadian currency would be the dime, not the dollar. Since dimes are one tenth the value of a dollar, the decimal point on every price could be moved over by one point and nothing else would have to change. The Canada-US exchange rate would no longer be 1.2 Canadian dollars per US dollar; rather, it would be 12 Canadian dimes per US dollar.

The world in which we live, being far from perfect, is one in which exchange rates matter a great deal. They matter precisely because goods are subject to significant trading costs which means that they need not have the same price when expressed in a common currency. Furthermore, many of the important prices in the economy appear to adjust slowly. That is, prices are somewhat rigid rather than perfectly flexible.

Variability in exchange rates probably matters most for the evaluation of investments. The decision to purchase a foreign asset depends on the present value of the stream of returns it will generate—expressed in home currency. Suppose we are in Canada considering the purchase of a factory in Mexico with a price of P Mexican Pesos (MXP). We are able to accurately forecast the Peso-denominated profit stream from this factory as π_t, where $t = 1, 2, 3, \ldots$ represents years from purchase time. We plan to spend the returns from our investment in Canada so we care about the Canadian dollar (CAD) value, V. Discounting at an interest rate of r, we obtain

$$V = -e_0 P + \sum_{t=1}^{\infty} \frac{e_t \pi_t}{(1+r)^t}.$$

In this expression e_0 is the exchange rate (CAD per MXP) at the time of purchase and e_t is the exchange in rate in future year t. Note that a permanent devaluation of the Peso ($e \Downarrow$) has two effects. First, it makes the purchase of the factory cheaper for us. Second, it lowers the returns. Indeed, since

$$(e\pi_t)/(eP) = \pi_t/P,$$

permanent exchange rate changes have no effect on the *prospective* return on assets —as long as they do not influence π_t.[1]

In practice, changes in exchange rates will affect profitability of foreign assets even as expressed in their own currency (π_t is measured in Pesos). The effect is complex and depends on the nature of the business. A depreciation will tend to confer a *competitive advantage* on the factory in Mexico. This will improve revenues from exports (in local currency units), lower competition from imports, but raise the price of inputs that must be imported (e.g. petroleum). It will also raise the domestic currency costs of any foreign debts. On the whole, manufacturing firms in a country tend to benefit from devaluations because their costs become more competitive relative to foreign producers. This may seem surprising since during an exchange rate crisis, even exporters may be suffering losses. The issue is that often a large fall in the currency is associated with a recession—because the government had pushed up interest rates to defend the currency or because foreign investors pull their money out—or rising inflation—because imported inputs become more expensive and this leads to across-the-board price increases. If exporters and import-competing firms could receive the benefits of the devaluation without the side effects of recession or inflation, they would be better off.

Future exchange rates must be forecast to calculate V. Is the current rate e_0 a good guide as to future rates? The answer depends in large part on the exchange rate system in place.

10.1 Exchange Rate Systems

Countries that let market forces alone determine their exchange rates operate a "pure" floating exchange rate system. Most governments per-

---

[1] If you are valuing an investment you purchased in the past, depreciations *will* affect return on assets if assets are expressed on a cost basis.

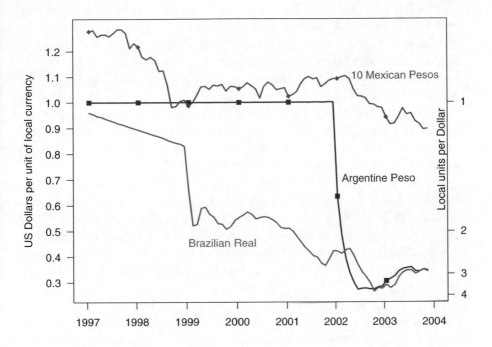

Fig. 10.1. Creeping, floating, and sinking exchange rates

ceive that market forces will lead to excess volatility and possibly to undesired valuations. As a result, they intervene in the exchange market to varying degrees. If the intervention is fairly limited, the system may be referred to as a "managed" or "dirty float." In such a system the central bank buys and sells foreign exchange and manipulates its home interest rate with the intent of keeping the exchange rate within certain *bands*. If the government uses very narrow bands and pursues them diligently, we refer to the system as a fixed or "pegged" exchange rate system. As we have seen in 1997 and 1998 in South-East Asia, Russia, and Brazil, the maintenance of fixed parities with the dollar may become infeasible if the exchange market actors bet aggressively against the currency. To ward off speculation Hong Kong and Argentina have tried to back their fixed exchange rate regimes with so-called "Currency Boards." The goal is to have enough foreign reserves so as to make an attack on the currency easily defensible. Hong Kong's peg to the U.S. dollar survived the Asia Crisis intact.

Argentina gave up its peg to the dollar and experienced a massive exchange rate depreciation in 2002, illustrated in Figure 10.1. Prior to that, the stable currency had been seen as a success story for currency boards. Brazil's exchange rate illustrates two different systems. During 1997 and 1998, it depreciated along a more or less straight line determined by the government to reflect differences in US and Brazilian inflation rates. I visited Brazil during that period and it seemed fairly clear that local prices were very high. This was because the initial peg rate was set too high. The result was that even though the currency was depreciating, the relative price of Brazilian goods remained too high, making it difficult for Brazilian exporters to compete and making imports very attractive. In early 1999, this so-called "creeping peg" became unsustainable and it was abandoned.

Figure 10.1 illustrates a very important principle. While "fixed" exchange rates do not vary much by definition, they are rarely permanent. Thus while Mexico seems the more "risky" currency in 1997 and 1998, underlying risks remained for Brazil and Argentina and then manifested themselves in the forms of sudden drops in 1999 and 2002, respectively. Thus, a fixed exchange rate regime retains exchange rate risk.

One way to fix the exchange rate with a greater degree of permanence is to abandon one's own currency and adopt the currency of another country. Panama and Ecuador use the US dollar as their currencies. Alternatively countries may collectively establish a new common currency. In 1999 eleven members of the European Union adopted a common currency called the Euro (*not* the "Eurodollar" as one occasionally hears).

For floating exchange rate systems, decades of econometric research have not been able to produce reliable exchange rate forecasting models. The best available predictor of the exchange rate tomorrow or a month from today or even a year from now is the current exchange rate. That does not mean that the exchange rate will not change over the next year. It almost surely will change—a lot. But it is just as likely to rise as it is to fall. While exchange rate fluctuations seem random in most cases, there are still some situations where we can see that certain fundamentals are going to be pressuring exchange rates in a certain direction. Eventually we believe exchange traders will yield to these fundamentals.

10.2 Fundamental Valuation

There is very little that would lend support to the Canadian dollar other than that it is massively undervalued on a fundamental

basis. *Robert Fairholm, Chief Canadian Economist, Standard &
Poors DRI.*

There was wide agreement that the Canadian dollar was significantly
undervalued in the late 1990s. In the mid-00s there is a similar consensus that the Chinese Renminbi is also undervalued. Indeed when the
Chinese set aside their rigid fix of the currency at 8.3 yuan/US$, the
Renminbi promptly appreciated. On the flip side, prior to the Real Crisis, there was a consensus that the Brazilian currency was *overvalued*.
Similar claims were made about the Mexican Peso in 1994 before the
Peso Crisis and about the US dollar in 1985 before the Plaza Accord
and again in 2005.

But what do over- and undervaluation really mean? How do we
determine whether a currency is incorrectly priced? We usually appeal
to two different, but related, *standards* of fundamental valuation. Before
we consider the arguments for exchange rates, it is worth building some
intuition from something we have more daily contact with: restaurants.
Suppose I say that Bistro X is overpriced. What sort of evidence would
I use to defend this claim? First, I might say Bistro X charges higher
prices for its main courses than do Bistros Y and Z. Second, I might
point out that Bistro X has many empty tables but Y and Z have lineups. The first claim follows from a "parity" standard and the latter
follows from an "equilibrium" standard.

10.2.1 Parity (Price) Standards

Parity standards work from the premise known as the Law of One Price
(LoOP). The "same thing" should not simultaneously trade for two different prices. If the same thing were available at two different prices,
consumers would only purchase from the cheaper source, forcing a decline in the price charged by the expensive supplier. Parity standards
are hypothetical exchange rates that would set prices of some good or
service to be equal in two different countries. Let us denote the home
country parity rate with the US dollar as $\bar{e}$. At that rate, we can convert home prices P^h into US dollars and they should be equal to the
foreign price P_f expressed in US dollars. Thus

$$\bar{e}P^h = P^f \quad \text{or, rearranging} \quad \bar{e} = P^f/P^h.$$

Is LoOP realistic? Yes, very much so, *if* we interpret "same thing"
very strictly. Two goods with exactly the same attributes, *including
location, time and manner of delivery*, should sell for the same price.

We see that in some organized commodity markets LoOP holds fairly closely. LoOP does not work well with the actual data we would use to calculate a parity standard.

Parity standards suffer from a number of well-known problems:

1. Most goods are "vertically differentiated." Thus the version of a good consumed in one country may have a higher price because it is higher quality than the version in the other country. It is particularly difficult to compare prices of "equivalent" houses, which is a problem since housing accounts for such a high share of the consumption bundle.
2. Many goods and most services are subject to high trade costs. This reduces the pressure to equalize prices in different locations.
3. Even for a highly tradeable good, we would want to compare wholesale prices because the retail markup is large and varies substantially across countries (e.g. high in Japan, low in the US).
4. Commodity taxes also induce differences in the prices consumers see, e.g. gas and cigarettes.

To address the quality issue, it is useful to compare prices of goods that we know to be essentially identical across countries. For example, consider the case of the "Miseducation of Lauryn Hill" CD (which won the Best Album Grammy in 1999). The US price (in Seattle) was US$17.99 whereas the Canadian price (Vancouver) was reported as C$19.09. This implies a compact disc price parity of 0.94 USD/CAD. At the exchange rates prevailing in 1999, the CD was 30% cheaper in Canada! This illustrates that even highly tradeable goods like compact disks do not obey the so-called Law of One Price.

Table 10.1 makes it clear that the parity exchange rate, column (3), depends very much on which good is used in the calculation. The article uses information from an article with the provocative title of "Cheap Dollar is Making Canada the Land of the Spree." At the time the article was written, the market exchange rate was 0.66 USD/CAD and the products reported upon were eight to 37% less expensive in Canada (once converted to a common currency). Using the exchange rates prevailing just prior to publication of this book, 0.93 USD/CAD, Canada's prices are generally higher than those in the US.

One famous case is the McDonalds Big Mac, which *The Economist* uses to calculate over/under-valuation according to "Big Mac Parity." The choice of the Big Mac seems strange given that is one of the least tradeable items one could imagine. However it has the advantage of being a well-recognized, mostly standardized good available in a large set of countries. For the most part, prices of the Big Mac appear to

Table 10.1. A border makes all the difference

	US Price (USD) P_{us} NY	Ca Price (USD) eP_{ca} ON	Parity (USD/CAD) P_{us}/P_{ca}	Gap $(eP_{ca} - P_{us})/P_{us}$
Sat. stay at Days Inn	$260.00	$165.00	1.04	-37%
Whopper at Burger King	$2.39	$2.18	0.72	-9%
	WA	BC		
Lauryn Hill CD	$17.99	$12.60	0.94	-30%
Nintendo 64 console	$130.00	$119.00	0.72	-8%
Starbucks latte	$2.70	$2.29	0.78	-15%
Levis 501 jeans	$50.00	$45.00	0.73	-10%

Note: Prices shown in USD, based on exchange rate of $e = 0.66$ USD/CAD.
Source: *New York Times*, August 1, 1999

reflect other prices in a country. However, there is no guarantee that this will be the case. Therefore looking at single product like the Big Mac can give a highly misleading signal. For example, in January 2006, a Big Mac cost 250 Yen in Japan. At the market rate of 114 Yen/USD, this gives a US dollar price of $2.19. Comparing to the average price in the US, $3.15, implies 31% undervaluation of the Yen.[2] Anyone who visited Japan in 2006 would report that prices there were not in general 31% lower than prices in the US.

To avoid the unrepresentative price behavior of single products, economists focus on averages over the prices of large numbers of goods and services. In particular, they use a measure called purchasing power parity (PPP). The price levels used for PPP calculations are the expenditure-weighted averages of all prices. According to PPPs in 2005, a bundle of goods and services that would cost $100 in the US would cost 12,900 Yen in Japan. The PPP rate is given by the ratio of these price levels, or 129 Yen/USD. Dividing the PPP rate by the market rate yields 1.13, implying a 13% *over-valuation* of the Yen.[3] Big Macs are, relatively speaking, a very good deal in Japan.

---

[2] Divide the price difference expressed in a common currency, $(2.19 - 3.15)$, by the US price to obtain $-.305$).

[3] Another way to reach the same conclusion is to divide the 12,900 Yen price level by the 114 Yen/USD market rate to find the price level in USD is $113.16. The $100 bundle is 13% more expensive in Japan.

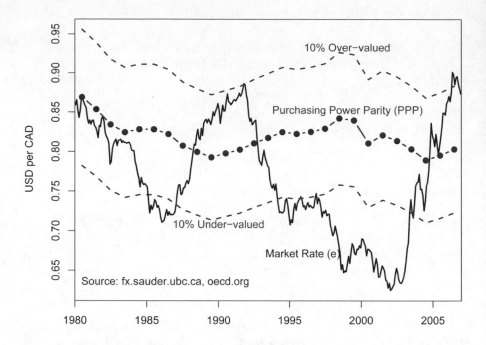

Fig. 10.2. Canada's market exchange rate with the US dollar compared various parity rates

Figure 10.2 compares the Canada-US market exchange rate with OECD estimates of the PPP exchange rate. We see that deviations from PPP are substantial and persistent. The dashed lines in the figure show that most of the time the CAD has not been more than 10% off of its PPP valuation. The data shown in this figure make it seem like one could make money by buying the CAD when it was under-valued and selling when over-valued. If you are sufficiently patient, it would probably work. However, the return towards PPP can take years and in the short-run the gap can get larger, as we see in the late 1990s. The extended period of undervaluation relative to PPP that Canada experienced then made it rather clear that free trade does not equalize all prices since Canada and the US had negligible tariffs on each other's imports by then.

There is a more severe problem with using PPP that Figure 10.2 does not illustrate. Canada and the US are at approximately the same level of development. Whenever we deal with the exchange rates between a poor and a wealthy country, we need to consider the "Penn Effect" illustrated in Figure 1.2. Recall that high income countries have a systematic tendency towards higher price levels. This means that we should not expect the exchange rate between Canada and India to move towards its PPP level. As long as India remains substantially poorer than Canada, its exchange rate will be undervalued relative to PPP.

Suppose we accept that at any given time there will be substantial deviations from PPP. This does not mean that there are no limits to possible deviations. One thing that has been found fairly generally is that a country with a high rate of inflation (say 20% or more per year) will usually experience a proportionate amount of depreciation relative to currencies that have low rates of inflation like the dollar. This regularity is sometimes referred to as "PPP in growth rates" or "relative PPP".

This idea can be better understood by using a little algebra. Suppose that, on average, the price level in the home country is systematically higher or lower than the price level in the foreign country (expressed in a common currency) by a factor k depending on relative incomes. If the home country is poor, then $k < 1$. It is convenient here to define the exchange rate as E, measured in local currency units per foreign currency unit. This is the reverse of the way we defined e up until now, i.e. $E = 1/e$. Defined this way, an increase in E is a *depreciation of the home currency*. Putting these ideas together we have

$$P_t^h = k_t E_t P_t^f.$$

If the same law holds last year as holds this year, then we divide home prices levels today, t, by those a year ago, $t - 1$ to obtain.

$$\frac{P_t^h}{P_{t-1}^h} = \frac{k_t}{k_{t-1}} \frac{E_t}{E_{t-1}} \frac{P_t^f}{P_{t-1}^f}.$$

Now, from year to year relative incomes do not change very much. This means $k_t \approx k_{t-1}$ so the fraction involving the k factors will cancel out. If we rearrange to focus on the market exchange rate we obtain:

$$\frac{E_t}{E_{t-1}} = \frac{P_t^h / P_{t-1}^h}{P_t^f / P_{t-1}^f}.$$

The left-hand side (LHS) of the equation is home *currency depreciation*. The right-hand side (RHS) is the ratio of *home price inflation* to *foreign price inflation*. To make things concrete, think of Bolivia in 1985. It was experiencing very high inflation compared to the US. If this were to continue with no change in the exchange rate, the prices of Bolivia's exports would soar as expressed in USD. Even if they started out cheap,

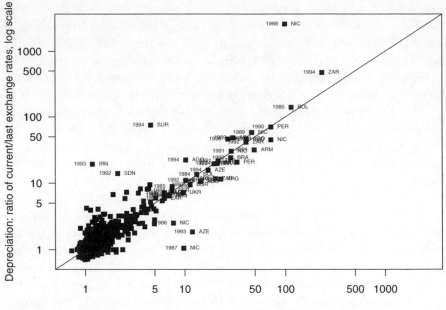

Fig. 10.3. Depreciation and inflation

they would quickly become much more expensive than other sources of the same products. This would force a depreciation of the Bolivian currency (the peso boliviano), which here corresponds to a rise in the LHS.

What all this means is that if relative prices in a common currency are not to change too much from year to year, then the LHS (depreciation) should keep close the the RHS (relative inflation). In a graph we would see home depreciation and relative inflation on a 45-degree line. To find out just how well this works in practice, I collected data from the World Bank's *World Development Indicators* from 1975 to 2004 and plotted more than 4000 annual differences in Figure 10.3.

Figure 10.3 reveals several things about exchange rate behaviour. First, the data do indeed line up well along the line with a slope of one.[4] This means that a country like Peru (PER in the figure) whose prices increased by a factor of 72 (over 40% per month!) from 1989 to 1990 relative to US inflation should have also experienced a depreciation by a factor of 72. Actual depreciation was by a factor of 70. One of

---

[4] I estimated the relationship using linear regression with both the LHS and RHS expressed in logs and obtained a slope of 0.999.

the anomalies from this relationship is Nicaragua in 1988 (center-top of figure). It shows much larger depreciation than the rate of inflation would seem to warrant. However, in two previous years (1986 and 1987) we see big reverse anomalies. Thus it would seem that in 1988, the Nicaraguan currency belatedly caught up by depreciating enough to correct for present and past inflations.

A second important point is that the strength of the linear relationship comes mainly from a relatively small portion of the data exhibiting very large inflation and depreciation rates. The majority of the data can be seen as a blur of points near the zeros of the figure. In this area the relationship between inflation and depreciation is much weaker.

The main take-away from the algebra and figure is that an economic force is at work, compelling price levels in different countries— expressed in a common currency—not to stray too far apart from each other. In cases of mild inflation, this force is not strong enough to overwhelm other forces pushing the exchange rate around. But when inflation is large enough, exchange rates have to adjust to prevent huge price disparities. Hyperinflation of this sort is relatively rare but the figure shows it does happen so it is something that we should be aware of, especially when conducting business with less developed economies. We now turn away from prices to focus on quantities as indicators that exchange rates have strayed from fundamentals.

10.2.2 Equilibrium (Quantity) Standards

Recall the relationship between exchange rates, comparative, and competitive advantage introduced in Chapter 2. In a simple world, without foreign ownership of domestic assets, the exchange rate would have to bring about equality in the value of imports and exports for each country. That is, an overvalued currency would be one in which the country persistently ran trade deficits with the rest of the world. As we saw in Chapter 2, equilibrium exchange rates give a country competitive advantages (lower unit costs in a common currency) in the industries in which it has comparative advantages. These ideas are more or less the same. If the currency were so low that a country had a competitive advantage in every industry, then it would be exporting, but not importing. The exports would create a supply of foreign exchange. Eventually the price of foreign exchange would have to decline to induce people to purchase it and import. If the currency were overvalued, then the country would be only importing. As the currency depreciated from an overvalued position, the first industries that would gain competitive advantage would be the comparative advantage industries because those are the ones where productivity is relatively high.

The current world economic system features significant cross-border asset ownership and this fact changes the equilibrium forces on the exchange rate. In particular, a country may import more than it exports if foreigners are willing to exchange goods for ownership of domestic assets such as cash, treasury bills, securities, or real estate. These assets generate a stream of future returns and the foreigner will presumably not be willing to forever reinvest its returns in more domestic assets. Eventually, they will want to use their income stream in domestic currency to purchase actual goods and services. Thus, another way of specifying fundamental valuation is that an exchange rate is correctly valued if it is consistent with *long-run* balanced trade. Put another way, a currency is overvalued if the country has an explosive debt path, i.e. if its obligations to provide income to the foreign owners of its assets are rising at such a rate that it will soon become impossible to finance these payments via export revenues. Lacking export revenue to pay interest on debts, one might try selling assets or borrowing more. However, eventually one runs out of assets to sell and creditors willing to lend to you. Then the only way to raise exports and lower imports so that you can generate more foreign exchange to pay off debts is to have home currency depreciation.

A good starting point in thinking about whether an exchange rate is overvalued or not is to examine the current supply and demand situation and speculate on how each element will develop in the future. Table 10.2 shows the main actors in exchange markets. Sellers of foreign exchange create the demand for local currency. When they are more active than buyers, the local currency will tend to appreciate.

Exporters and importers account for only about one percent of the volume of currencies exchanged each year. The main source of sales and purchases of foreign exchange is purchases of assets such as land, corporate stock, and treasury bills. Before we can accurately predict exchange rates we will probably have to develop better models explaining these financial motivations.

Interest rates are an important part of the equilibrium mechanisms. Canada's sole period of overvaluation in PPP terms relative to the US$ in the last two decades came from 1989–91 when it had sharply higher interest rates than the US (as much as five percentage points). To fend off attacks on their currencies, many countries try raising interest rates. This makes their treasury bills more attractive to foreign investors. It also discourages speculators from borrowing domestic currency and

Table 10.2. Actors in the foreign currency (exchange) market

		Foreign exchange	
		Sellers	Buyers
Balance of Payments Account	Current:	exporters, recipients of foreign income	importers, payers of foreign income
	Capital:	inward investors, outward investors, currency market speculators	
	Reserves:	central banks	

then using it to buy foreign exchange. Nevertheless, it should be noted that interest rate gaps are not strong predictors of short-run exchange rate changes.

Declines in the Canadian dollar in the late 1990s and rises in the mid-2000s were widely attributed to movements of world commodity prices. The following equilibrium story seems to be at work. Canada exports large amounts of resource-based commodities (wheat, potash, lumber). When demand for them declines we see lower export volumes and lower prices per unit. The resulting fall in foreign exchange earnings reduces the supply of foreign exchange (US dollars), leading to a rise in their price, which means a depreciation in the Canadian dollar. Another way to tell the story is that with exports of commodities declining, Canada must find offsetting gains in exports of manufactured goods. This requires lower relative compensation for Canadian workers in the manufacturing sector.

An example of equilibrium analysis that correctly predicted exchange rate changes is contained in a speech given by economist Paul Krugman in Mexico City in May 1993. During the early 1990s, Mexico had a growing current account deficit. Its imports were able to grow faster than exports because of large inflows of foreign capital. Krugman said, "Mexico has been the target, not so much of a rational appreciation of its strengths by international investors, as of a sudden irrational financial infatuation...But there is a looming short- or medium-term problem: unless capital inflows continue at six percent of [gross domestic product] a year, the peso is greatly overvalued...I expect, and welcome, a Mexican devaluation." The capital inflows Krugman refers to are the counterpart of Mexico's current account deficit. The presumption is that borrowing of six percent of your total income (Gross Domestic Product) is not sustainable. One and a half years later, the peso fell suddenly from 6.5 per dollar to 10 per dollar in few months. The equilibrium analysis that growing current account deficits could not be sustained was born out in practice. While it is possible to construct such stories after the fact and occasionally fixed exchange rates are sufficiently misaligned to successfully predict a collapse, no one has managed to implement the equilibrium approach in a way that reliably predicts floating exchange rates.

10.3 Responses to Exchange Rate Risk

If we accept that the unpredictable changes are an inherent part of most exchange rate regimes, then we must move to the question of how to respond to the risks associated with exchange rate volatility.

Exchange rate risk is the chance that a movement in the exchange rate will have negative effects on the profitability of the "exposed" firm. One way to lower exchange rate risk—that is, to reduce exchange rate exposure—is to use financial instruments, often referred to as "hedges." This is a large and complex topic that would be considered in depth in a course on international financial management. For now let's focus on just two simple ideas.

- Use forward contracts: If you know in advance that you will receive certain revenue flows in foreign currency, you can buy domestic currency forward. This locks you into a fixed exchange rate to convert those revenues. There are limits to the use of this approach. First, forward contracts may not be available for certain currencies, in particular less developed economies. Second, purchasers may not be willing to commit far into the future for purchases. Economic conditions in other countries may give a competitive advantage to a rival producer. Your customer may then switch suppliers.
- Denominate debt in same currency as major revenue source: Suppose the firm exports are mainly destined to Europe. Then home appreciation will likely reduce export revenues and home depreciation will increase them. To hedge we need a separate item that moves in the opposite direction. One possibility is to borrow from a European bank. In that case home appreciation will lower the home currency required to make interest payments. Thus when export revenues fall there is also a fall in debt servicing costs, and costs rise when export revenues rise. This dampens the movement in profits.

Political Risk

Economic considerations, such as a country's factor endowments, its workers' wages and productivities, and the industrial agglomerations it houses are fundamental considerations in evaluating the profitability of a nation as a potential investor. However, it is equally vital to consider the policies of the host-government. In this chapter, I first discuss a more traditional manner of treating political issues which I refer to as "analysis." This corresponds to a setting where political events are part of the exogenous environment of international investment. Next I turn to the cases where the multinational enterprise realizes that its actions can actually influence political outcomes. It can take strategic decisions to lead to preferred results.

11.1 Political Analysis

Political analysis is like forecasting the weather: you know the force you are studying has a major influence on your well-being but you also know that you cannot hope to have any reciprocal influence on it. There are three approaches one can take:

Forecast and Avoid: Try to identify which countries are relatively safe from the point of view of stable governments. Stay out of the unsafe countries. This is actually very difficult. For instance, "stability" is not an easy concept to define. In some countries the particular set of government leaders may change frequently without any dramatic changes in the basic form and conduct of the government. For example, the *Economist* reported on February 22, 2007 that Italy had just formed its 61st government since 1945. Other countries, like Indonesia under Sukarno (President from 1945 to 1967) and Suharto

(1967–1998), have dictators that remain in power for decades. However, such countries can have underlying political problems that lead to revolutionary change. Before Sukarno was removed, conflict resulted in the deaths of an estimated half a million Indonesians. Italy had posed fewer political risks than Indonesia from 1945–2000 even though Indonesia exhibited fewer political changes.

The astute political forecaster must first determine the range of political scenarios. Then she must try to assign some probability to each one. The second task is necessarily imprecise but both tasks can be very useful exercises because they focus the investor on the fact that status quo is not inevitable. Indeed, under close examination, one can realize that the status quo is not even sustainable.

Rapid Evacuation: If you are in an area where risk is high, be prepared to pull out as soon as a crisis emerges. It is crucial to maintain up-to-date political "intelligence." This approach also requires that you not invest heavily in immobile capital equipment. Rather, key assets should be retractable (equipment that can be easily sold or removed at short notice).

Insure: When, as is often the case, it is impossible to predict political troubles accurately, and there is no real way to avoid investments in immobile assets, the firm may try to insure them. For American firms there is the option of insuring through the Overseas Private Investment Corporation (OPIC). Firms from other countries can seek out private insurers such as Lloyds (which has insured against a variety of political risks—including the capture of merchant ships by vessels of enemy nations—for centuries). The World Bank offers insurance against events like expropriation, revolution, war, and terrorism through its Multilateral Investment Guarantee Agency (MIGA).

While insurance is an option in principle, it does not solve all the practical problems of political risk. Premiums may be high and insurers may refuse to cover certain investments. More fundamentally, insurance requires a verifiable "event" that causes a payout. Governments rarely engage in overt nationalization of the property of a foreign firm. However they sometimes undertake a series of actions that have the cumulative effect of destroying the value of the firm's investment. This is referred to as "creeping expropriation[1]" It is generally very hard to insure against. Firms need to respond to the threat of creeping expropriation by conceiving and executing a *political strategy*.

---

[1] For additional discussion see August (1997).

11.2 Political Strategy

The term strategy can mean different things in different contexts. Here what I mean is that the multinational firm acts with an awareness that the host government's actions will in part depend on the firm's actions. That is, firm and government are interdependent. The political strategy approach views firm-government relations as a kind of game. At each point the two "players" actively attempt to manipulate their positions in a struggle over who will capture the potential surplus associated with the MNE's investment.

11.2.1 Understand Host-Country Objectives

What do host country governments really want from the foreign investor? Traditionally, they have sought out a fairly constant set of perceived benefits. While the relative importance attached to each item varies across countries and circumstances, the following are viewed positively:

- Government revenues: At a basic level, of the value added by the subsidiary, the host government would like to take a higher share in revenues for the government (and possibly corrupt regulators or tax collectors) rather than letting it be repatriated to foreign shareholders.
- Job creation: Firms care not just about the number of workers employed (which may be rather small in comparison to the size of the host labour force) but also to the *location* of the workers and the *skills* involved. Other things equal, the host government would like to see job creation in backwards or depressed regions within the nation rather than the capital city. Furthermore, it would like jobs that pay high wages and add to the demand for skilled workers while also adding to supply by training workers in new skills.
- Technology transfer: new processes that raise the skills of domestic workers and enhance capabilities of domestic supply firms.
- Capital: funds that might not otherwise have been available to purchase manufacturing plant and equipment.
- Improved trade balance: Host governments often attach perversely high benefits to export revenues and reductions in import expenses. Thus, they often (China is a prime example) want firms to see foreign countries as their primary market rather than the host country market. If a firm does serve the home country market, it is preferred that it be replacing a previously foreign source of supply. Furthermore they would prefer that firms purchase domestically produced

inputs rather than imported materials. There are probably three sources for this preference. First, there is the longstanding influence of the doctrine of mercantilism where exporting more than you import is seen as good in itself. Second, many less developed countries keep overvalued exchange rates which puts them in a position of a chronic shortage of foreign exchange. Third, the domestic governments are often reluctant to create extra competition for domestic suppliers. By exporting or import substituting, the foreign firm is thought to be primarily competing with other foreign firms.

11.2.2 Catalogue Host-Country Policy Instruments

How do they achieve the goals described above? Governments use a myriad of policies, of course, but here I focus on the ones that try to compel the MNE to do things it would not otherwise want to do.

- Government revenues: high taxes, restrictions on repatriations of dividends, bureaucratic processes that tend to trigger bribes.
- Technology transfer: maximum foreign ownership rules that force the MNE to co-own the subsidiary with a local firm.
- Job creation: minimum employment requirements, policies that make it difficult to employ expatriate managers, tax incentives based on location of factory in high-unemployment regions.
- Capital: since FDI involves by definition the inflow of capital, this is usually not an area where government policy is in conflict with the MNE's interests.
- Improved trade balance: export requirements, minimum domestic content rules, exchange rate balancing. Actions of this sort are referred to by the World Trade Organization as Trade Related Investment Measures (TRIMs).

11.2.3 Calculate Host-Country Bargaining Power

How much scope does a host government have to extract surplus from an MNE? In many cases, competition among host-governments to attract FDI is fierce enough that the MNE is in position to obtain concessions rather than give them away. However, three types of circumstances shift bargaining power in favour of the host:

- Large home market. The foreign firm does not want to leave large sets of consumers completely unserved. Even if the margins are small, a sufficiently populous or wealthy nation may be too attractive for a company to pass up.

- Scarce Resource. Countries like the Arab states with their oil or many other countries with reserves of precious metals are also in a good bargaining position with the MNE.
- Investments that are country-specific and irreversible. This implies that the MNE that is mistreated cannot simply walk away with their assets. Rather, much or all of the value of the investment is lost if the MNE tries to exit. This is very much analogous to the relationship-specific investment introduced in Chapter 8.

The first-two circumstances imply that the host-country has some unique attribute that gives it *ex-ante* power in the negotiation process. The third circumstance affects *ex-post* bargaining power because it means that the outside option if bargaining breaks down is not very attractive to the firm.

11.2.4 Enhance the Firm's Own Strategic Position

Most nations now regard multinational investments as a net positive influence on the local economy. Thus, they want to attract investment in the first place and avoid exits by dissatisfied MNEs. However, to the extent possible, most governments would prefer to give lower subsidies and receive higher taxes from the MNE. The firm, on the other hand, would like to use the threat to close its local plant as a way to compel the host government to treat it favourably. The extent that such threats will work depends in large part on both sides' understanding of the "payoffs."

In the game-tree in Figure 11.1 we illustrate the possibility of a threat that the host-government may not find credible. The MNE threatens to close its plant if it does not receive a subsidy of $10 million. The gross economic benefit of the plant to the host country (as perceived by the government, at least) is $17m. Hence, if that were the outcome, the firm would be very happy and the government would also receive a surplus of $7m. However, if the government has full information, it will see that if there is no subsidy, the MNE will still prefer a payoff of -5 to one of -15. Hence even if denied the subsidy the MNE would still keep the plant open. Thus, its threat to depart unless it receives the subsidy is not credible. Therefore the government should just ignore it and end up at its preferred outcome (plant open, no subsidy) where the payoff is 17.

The MNE wants to reach the node of the tree where it keeps the plant open *and* receives a subsidy. How can the MNE change the structure of the game to accomplish this goal?

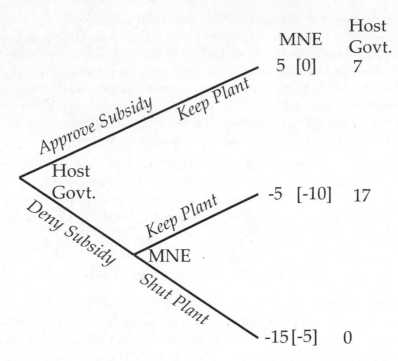

Fig. 11.1. Is the MNE's threat credible?

Alternatives: Try to preserve the option to walk away by avoiding large
sunk investments in immobile country-specific assets. Instead invest
in retractable assets. Also, invest outside the home country in creating *strategic alternatives*. An alternative is strategic if you do not
actually intend to ever use it but rather hope that the mere existence of the alternative will persuade the other party to act in a way
that favours your interests. For instance, if you establish a plant in
Thailand, buy some land in Malaysia to signal your willingness and
ability to leave Thailand and put your factory in Malaysia instead.
The idea is illustrated in the game tree in Figure 11.1 with the new
payoffs in square brackets for the MNE. Note that the alternative
makes it less costly to close the plant (-5 instead of -15). However,
the cost is that profits of keeping the plant open are now lower. This
is because the cost of the strategic alternative must be born even
if it is not used (like an insurance premium). The creation of the
strategic alternative now makes closing the plant more attractive
if there is no subsidy. Thus the threat becomes credible (the MNE
prefers -5 to -10). Since the host government prefers 7 to 0, it will

now provide the subsidy in order to keep the plant open. The MNE ends up just breaking even but this is still better than the loss of $5m it would have experienced had it not invested in the strategic alternative. Thus the mere existence of the alternative changes the outcome of the strategic interaction even though the firm does not actually take the alternative in the equilibrium.

Delay: In many cases, it is necessary to place immobile assets in a country where the assets are at risk of expropriation. One way to maintain bargaining power under such circumstances is to engage in *strategic delay*. This is where the firm postpones investments in new technologies or expanded capacity longer than is desirable from a pure business point of view. Knowing you have the option of not investing at all in the future if you feel you were ill-treated, you now have a "carrot" to dangle in front of the host-government to induce it to treat you well.

Friendship: Invest in making friends with politically influential citizens of the host nation. While it may backfire, you should also cultivate contacts with politicians in the home country government, especially if your home country has a fair amount of political influence with the host country.

Reputation: Sometimes the only way to punish a host-government for a negative action is to do something that actually hurts your interests as well. Suppose for instance you are forced to give half the equity of a subsidiary to a member of the ruling elite. This amounts to a 50% expropriation. However keeping the remaining 50% and the associated stream of profits might be better than nothing. Nevertheless, it may pay to terminate the investment immediately, especially if your participation is vital to making the subsidiary profitable. Not only will the host-government see that you are "tough" but other potential hosts will observe that you retaliate even if it does not serve your short-run interests. Such behaviour is obviously costly but for certain firms it is worth the effort to develop a reputation as a company that cannot be pushed around.

References

August, Ray, 1997, *International Business Law*, Prentice Hall.

Encarnation, Dennis and Sushil Vachani, 1985, "Foreign Ownership: When Hosts Change the Rules," *Harvard Business Review* September/October, pp. 152–160.

Poynter, Thomas, 1986, "Managing Government Intervention: A Strategy for Defending the Subsidiary," *Columbia Journal of of World Business,* Winter, pp. 55–65.

12

International Taxation

Taxes have the potential to create substantial differences in the attractiveness of doing business in two otherwise equal locations. Firms doing business abroad are subject to a variety of taxes including payroll taxes, sales taxes, income taxes and withholding taxes. In this chapter, I will focus on the last two since they present the most complications. Discussion of personal income taxes will be deferred to the chapter on staffing of overseas affiliates. Thus, the focus here is on how nations tax a firm's profits.

12.1 Jurisdiction: Who Taxes Whom

There are three important principles of taxing income: source, residence, and nationality. Virtually all countries tax income sourced (earned) within their borders. Corporations and "natural" persons have a residency (usually their permanent address). Most developed countries tax their residents on their world-wide income and tax non-residents on their income earned within the country. The US deems the worldwide income of its citizens to be subject to US income tax, no matter where they reside. It seems to be the only country to tax individuals on the basis of nationality. The upshot of these overlapping tax jurisdictions is that residents of one country earning income in another source country often find themselves subject to tax on that income in both the home country and the source country (where the business was conducted). If the same income is actually taxed twice, it is called *double taxation*.

In order to reduce double taxation, most developed and many less developed countries have negotiated *tax treaties* with each other. These treaties override domestic law. Treaties normally follow a model suggested by the OECD. They place limitations on one country's right to tax residents of the other country. One important limitation is that a company doing business in another country is not subject to tax in that other country unless the company has a *permanent establishment* in that country. Thus, a company can export into a particular country without being subject to income taxes in that country provided the company does not set up an office or fixed place of business in the country. If there are no significant business advantages associated with creating a permanent establishment, then from a tax perspective, it is probably a good idea not to have one in high tax countries.

12.2 Simple Algebra of International Taxation

International tax rules can be fiendishly complex in practice. Our goal here is understand some of the basic principles involved. This is necessarily a simplified version of what happens in the real world, especially since tax systems vary considerably from country to country. However, an understanding of the basic ideas should help you to make some sense of what is going on in specific situations.

We start with an entity (it could be a person or a corporation) that earns income in the country of residence, called H for home, and in a foreign country called F. Worldwide income (Y_W) comprises home (Y_H) and foreign (Y_F) source income: $Y_W = Y_H + Y_F$. World tax payments, $T_W = T_H + T_F$, are the sum of taxes paid to home (T_H) and foreign (T_F) governments.

If all countries taxed fixed proportions of the local *source* income, life would be simple. The entity would pay $T_H = t_H Y_H$ to the home government and $T_F = t_F Y_F$ to the foreign government, where t_H and t_F are flat tax rates. Worldwide tax obligations would be just $T_W = t_H Y_H + t_F Y_F$.

The normal situation is that the home country taxes you (as a resident) on your worldwide income and the foreign country taxes just foreign source income. The resulting tax obligations would start out as $T_H = t_H Y_W$ and $T_F = t_F Y_F$. This would lead to a total tax obligation of

$$T_W = \underbrace{t_H(Y_H + Y_F)}_{T_H} + \underbrace{t_F Y_F}_{T_F} = t_H Y_H + (t_H + t_F)Y_F$$

This equation shows the double taxation of foreign income. It is shown graphically as the higher dashed line in Figure 12.1. The figure shows how rising foreign tax rates increase the total tax of the entity.

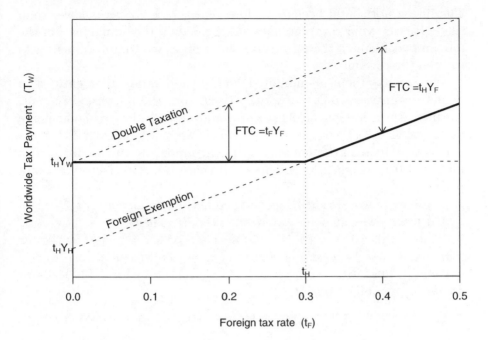

Fig. 12.1. Tax credits and exemptions

To alleviate the burden of double taxation, most countries offer income exemptions and/or foreign tax credits. Exemptions mean that some foreign income is excluded from tax at home.[1] If all foreign income is exempt, then we are back to the world of source-based taxation since $T_H = t_H(Y_W - Y_F) = t_H Y_H$ and $T_F = t_F Y_F$. This case is shown in Figure 12.1 with the lower of the two straight dashed lines.

Foreign tax credits (FTC) allow the entity to deduct an amount based on taxes paid abroad from the amount it would otherwise owe the home government. Thus, $T_H = t_H Y_W - \text{FTC}$. If taxes are lower in the foreign country, then the FTC is just the amount of taxes the entity actually paid the foreign government, i.e. $t_F Y_F$. This case is shown with the horizontal segment of the solid line in Figure 12.1 to the left of the dotted vertical line corresponding to equal tax rates ($t_F = t_H$). Total tax obligations are

$$T_W = T_H + T_F = [t_H Y_H + t_H Y_F - t_F Y_F] + t_F Y_F = t_H Y_H + t_H Y_F = t_H Y_W.$$

---

[1] For example, the US taxes its citizens on their world income but excludes the first eighty thousand dollars of earned income in the foreign country if it deems the citizen to be a *bona fide* resident of that country.

The line is horizontal because as long as the foreign tax is lower than the home tax, your total tax does not depend on the actual level of the foreign tax. Instead, the foreign tax determines which government gets to keep the revenue.

If $t_F > t_H$ then an unlimited FTC would imply that entities in high t_F countries would get money back from the home government. An increase in foreign income, Y_F, would actually lower higher home tax payments, T_H! Not surprisingly this is *not* the way the FTC works in practice. Instead the home government limits the tax credit so that FTC $\leq$ LIM, where LIM is defined as the product of factors (a) and (b):

(a) share of worldwide income earned in the foreign country (Y_F/Y_W)

(b) taxes owed at home *before* the FTC $(t_H Y_W)$

Thus, LIM = (a) × (b) = $(Y_F/Y_W) \times (t_H Y_W) = t_H Y_F$, or *the tax that would have been paid on the foreign income if it had been earned at home*. Thus, if $t_F > t_H$ then FTC = LIM = $t_H Y_F$. This leads to domestic tax obligations of

$$T_H = t_H Y_w - \text{LIM} = t_H Y_H + t_H Y_F - t_H Y_F = t_H Y_H,$$

and worldwide tax payments of

$$T_w = t_H Y_H + t_F Y_F.$$

This is the same equation as we found under the system of a foreign income exemption.

Combining the two cases, the total tax payment is shown in Figure 12.1 as the kinked (like a hockey stick) solid line. To the right of the dotted vertical line, FTC=LIM which is less than tax actually paid to the foreign government. The difference between the tax paid, $t_F Y_F$ and the LIM is sometimes called the "excess foreign tax credits." In the figure it is given by the vertical distance between the hockey-stick line and the horizontal dashed line.[2]

Table 12.1 provides two examples. In panel (a), the home country has higher taxes and in panel (b), it has lower taxes. In both cases the firm's worldwide income is $100m, of which $40m is host-source income.

In the first frame, when home has the higher of the two rates, we see that the entity has a total tax obligation of $30m, which means

---

[2] In some more complex versions of the FTC system, the excess foreign tax credits can be added to the FTC available in other tax years or other foreign tax jurisdictions when that FTC would otherwise lie below the limit. This is not relevant in the one-foreign-country one-year case we are considering in this section.

Table 12.1. A comparison of taxes when home is the high (30%) and low (20%) jurisdiction

Nation	Income source	Income taxable	Tax Rate	Tax b.c.	Credits.	Tax a.c.
(a)						
Home	60	100	30%	30	8	22
Foreign	40	40	20%	8	0	8
World	100		30%			30
(b)						
Home	60	100	20%	20	8	12
Foreign	40	40	30%	12	0	12
World	100		24%			24

that it is paying an average tax rate of 30% on its world income. In the lower frame the average tax rate has fallen to 24%. What about the idea that under tax credits you pay the higher of the two rates? Keep in mind that this applies only to the income subject to both taxes, that is the foreign-source income. The table makes it a little tricky to see what is going on with foreign-source income. A quick calculation tells us that $18m of the $22m in home taxes in panel (a) were due to home income. Thus total tax on foreign income is $12m or 30%. In panel (b), all $12m of home taxes is for home-source income. The total tax on foreign income remains $12m (30%) in panel (b)—even though the allocation between taxation authorities has changed considerably. Under the simple FTC, foreign income ends up being taxed at the higher of the two rates, but it is not double taxed.

12.3 Taxation of MNCs' Earnings from Abroad

The taxation of foreign businesses depends on the type of legal entity involved. If a corporation operates directly within a foreign country without incorporating, the foreign operation is a *branch*. A branch is not separate from the parent; it is part of the same entity. If a corporation sets up an entity that is incorporated in a foreign country, it is a foreign *subsidiary*. The foreign subsidiary is a *separate legal entity* from the parent. Other legal forms include partnerships and joint ventures. However, what business-people call a joint venture is usually not a joint venture under the legal definition. Most "joint ventures" (in business language) are incorporated and are therefore subsidiaries (in legal terms).

Generally, tax is imposed on an entity basis. If a Canadian company sets up a subsidiary in Chile, and the Chilean subsidiary (a resident of Chile) carries on business only in Chile, then only Chile taxes the earnings of the Chilean subsidiary. If instead, the Canadian company sets up a branch in Chile, then the earnings of the branch are subject to both Canadian and Chilean tax. If losses are expected in the early stages, it may be a good idea to set up a branch, since the losses could be used to reduce Canadian taxes. There are exceptions to the general rule of taxing only on an entity basis.

Branch income is taxed when it is earned by the host government based on the source principle and the home government based on the residence principle. Home governments generally offer tax credits to avoid double taxation of the branches earnings.

Subsidiaries are distinct legal entities and their tax obligations depend on the home country. Each country has its own approach to taxing a MNE's dividends from its foreign subsidiaries. The US, the UK, Japan, and a few other countries mainly use foreign tax credit systems. In principle, they tax the dividends as though the parent earned the foreign income directly and then offer a foreign tax credit with respect to income taxes paid by the subsidiary (plus withholding taxes paid on the dividend payment). I wrote "in principle" in the last sentence for a reason: the tax rules on multinational earnings are very complex. For example, US firms can delay tax on active business income earned by overseas subsidiaries until they actually repatriate the income. This delay decreases the present value of tax obligations. Furthermore, when home governments allow tax credits to be calculated using foreign tax averaging, the MNC can apply its excess tax credits from foreign countries with high taxes to other foreign countries with low taxes.[3] The bottom line is that FTC systems for multinational subsidiaries do not work in practice as the simple FTC case we studied in the previous section. Even firms headquartered in FTC-based home countries often find tax advantages from moving income to low-tax areas.

Many countries offer exemptions to resident multinationals that cover most or all of the income earned by their overseas subsidiaries. Important examples of countries that offer exemption systems include Australia, Belgium, Canada, France, Germany, Italy, and the Nether-

---

[3] Hines (2004, pp. 6–8) provides a longer discussion of these points.

lands.[4] Again the rules are inevitably complex. For example, the Canadian system of taxing dividends received from abroad depends on

1. the degree of ownership,
2. the type of income, and
3. which country the income comes from.

Dividend income on portfolio investments is subject to regular Canadian tax. Portfolio investments are those in which the shareholder owns less than 10% of the shares. A foreign tax credit can be claimed in Canada for taxes paid abroad (including withholding taxes to be discussed later).

The rules, however, are different for dividends received from foreign affiliates (foreign corporations in which the investor owns at least 10% of any class of shares). Income from an active business earned by a foreign affiliate in a treaty-country (i.e. a country with which Canada has a tax treaty) is *exempt* from Canadian tax. Suppose, for example, CanCo sets up a wholly-owned subsidiary (which is a foreign affiliate) in Portugal (which is a treaty-country). The subsidiary sells CanCo's products (which is an active business) and then pays dividends to the Canadian parent company. That dividend income is totally exempt from Canadian income tax. This makes it seem like firms based in exemption systems like the Canadian one have big incentives to move income to low tax countries. As with the FTC systems studied above, we can not really draw this simple conclusion because countries like Canada tend to limit the application of exemptions to other countries with similar tax rates.

Income from an active business earned in a *non-treaty* country is subject to tax when a dividend is paid. As with passive income, FTCs are available to avoid double taxation. For example, suppose CanCo sets up a subsidiary in Hong Kong (a non-treaty country, even though China is a treaty country). The subsidiary sells CanCo's products and pays a 15% income tax. Suppose CanCo's normal Canadian tax rate is 45%. Upon receiving a dividend from Hong Kong, it will pay Canadian tax on the original income earned in Hong Kong. The Canadian tax will be such that the total taxes on the business income will add up to 45% (approximately). Of that amount, the Hong Kong government receives 15%, and the Canadian government receives 30%. However, the Canadian tax does not apply until the income is repatriated to Canada.

---

[4] This list comes from Hines (2004).

12.4 Withholding Taxes

In addition to applying business income tax rates to business income, most countries impose withholding taxes on certain types of payments to non-residents. Payments subject to withholding taxes usually include dividends, interest, royalties, and management fees. Since these are the main ways that multinationals extract profits from their overseas investments, the withholding tax can be thought of as a kind of tax on owning assets abroad, similar to the way import duties are a tax on international trade.

According to the Canadian Income Tax Act, such payments to non-residents are subject to a 25% withholding tax. However, in practice the 25% rate rarely applies, because most tax treaties set upper limits to withholding tax rates. The upper limits tend to be in the 5% to 15% range. Since each tax treaty is different, the withholding rates can vary, depending on which countries are involved.

The withholding tax, at rate r_F, is paid after corporate income taxes have been applied. Thus total taxes paid to the foreign government are given by

$$T_F = \underbrace{t_F Y_F}_{\text{income}} + \underbrace{r_F(1 - t_F)Y_F}_{\text{withholding}} = [t_F + r_F(1 - t_F)]Y_F.$$

The effective foreign income tax *rate* becomes $t_F^* = t_F + r_F(1-t_F)$. For example, if the corporate rate were 40% and the withholding tax were 10%, then the total share of foreign income paid to foreign government is $0.4 + 0.1(1 - 0.4) = 46\%$.

As tax treaties normally do not eliminate withholding taxes altogether, we still potentially have some double taxation. Withholding taxes can potentially trigger double taxation in two ways:

1. Business income that is repatriated to a parent is taxed first at business income tax rates and then again on the repatriation of the dividend.
2. Payments subject to withholding taxes can also be subject to regular income taxes in the country of the recipient.

Tax credits are potentially available at home for the withholding tax paid to the foreign government. As before, the FTC would be the lesser of taxes paid $(t_F^* Y_F)$ and home taxes payable $(t_H Y_F)$. There are no credits for withholding taxes under an exemption system since the foreign income in that case was not taxable at home.

12.5 Tax Reduction Strategies

The goal of tax strategy is to maximize after-tax world profits $(Y_W - T_W)$ subject to the constraint of not to being convicted of tax evasion and sent to jail. This means that tax strategy can be thought of as the search for ways to *legally* lower taxes (T_W) without reducing pre-tax income (Y_W).

Recall that under exemption systems, after-tax global profits are given by

$$Y_W - T_W = Y_W - (t_H Y_H + t_F^* Y_F) = Y_W[1 - t_F^* + s(t_F^* - t_H)],$$

where $s \equiv Y_H/Y_W$ is the home share of world income and t_F^* is the foreign tax rate including the effect of withholding taxes. Examining this equation, we see that we can raise after-tax profits by increasing s (i.e. redistribute income to the headquarters) whenever effective foreign tax rates are higher than home rates. When home tax rates are higher, we want to decrease s so as to reallocate income to low-tax treaty countries.

Under FTC systems we still want to raise s when foreign taxes are higher than home taxes. But under the FTC there is less of an incentive to move income to low-tax foreign countries because the higher home tax rate will still apply to foreign income. Nevertheless, due to payment delay and foreign tax averaging, there may still be tax gains from moving income to low-tax foreign countries.

The question then is how to actually move s around without breaking any laws. We have already considered two possible tax reduction strategies: exporting (which avoids the creation of a permanent establishment) and the branch form for investments abroad that are expected to earn losses during their early days. Following we consider three more strategies. We should note upfront that tax authorities do not make it easy for any of these strategies to be used extensively. Furthermore, these strategies may result in business disadvantages that more than offset any tax gains.

12.5.1 Transfer Pricing

Whenever one entity sells a good or service to another entity, there must be a price. When the entities are related corporations, the price is called a transfer price. Transfer pricing is an issue in the sale of goods, the provision of services by head office, and royalty charges between related corporations.

Let's consider a specific example. Suppose we have a Headquarters (HQ) that sells engines to a foreign affiliate (FA) that assembles and sells cars. The HQ charges FA a transfer price for each engine. Income at home includes the revenue from selling the engines to the FA. Meanwhile, the FA's income deducts the amount paid for the engines it obtains from HQ. Summing up, the MNC's world income does not depend on the level of the transfer price. However, the transfer price *does* affect T_W because it determines the share of income earned at home, s. The multinational benefits from a high transfer price when the foreign income tax rate is high.

Unfortunately for the MNC, tax law requires that transfer prices be set at arm's length values. Fortunately for tax-reduction strategists, arm's length values for internal transactions are usually difficult to determine. Usually, there is a range of prices which could reasonably be justified to the tax authorities.

In the past, many companies set an arbitrary price and then waited until the tax auditor knocked on the door before bothering to figure out how to justify the price. Moreover, penalties for using inappropriate prices had previously been light. During the 1990s the United States government believed that Japanese companies' American profits were being reported at levels that were unreasonably low. As a result, the US introduced more specific rules on how to compute transfer prices. It also established severe penalties for failure to properly document how the firm decided upon its transfer prices. Canada has introduced similar rules requiring documentation to be in place. Despite these rules, transfer prices cannot be determined without some subjective judgment. As a result, there can be considerable disagreement over what the fair price should be. Resolving disagreement usually involves negotiation.

Resolving a transfer price problem can be problematic since a MNC may need to negotiate with two or more governments. One government will want a high price and another government will want a low price, and the MNC is caught in the middle. In the past, it had been fairly easy for a MNC to push prices towards a tax-optimal result. The MNC generally had an advantage in negotiation since it knew its own business very well, while the government knew very little. Governments have recently recognized the enormous potential for tax dollars in the area, and have significantly increased focus and expertise in auditing transfer prices. Despite the opportunities and risks associated with transfer pricing, many MNCs continue to use simple mark-ups without adequate

justification or thought. These MNCs apparently believe the benefits
of a careful study do not exceed the costs.

One thing to keep in mind is that the transfer prices used for tax
purposes do not have to be the same ones used for internal management purposes. That is, somewhat surprisingly, it is legal to keep two
sets of books. This is very important because you would not want to
penalize the manager of a subsidiary in a high-tax country for her low
profits if those profits were low because of the high transfer prices that
management were forcing her to pay. The concern I would have about
using the two-books policy is that a tax auditor might use your management book to argue that the transfer prices in the tax book were
distorted.

*Before devising your own transfer pricing system, you should defi-
nitely seek expert legal advice.*

12.5.2 Thin Capitalization

Another way of lowering taxes when investing in a high tax country
is to finance the subsidiary with debt rather than equity. That way
normal earnings will be repatriated in the form of interest rather than
dividends. Interest will be expensed in the foreign country, lowering pre-
tax profit there. The interest revenue will be taxed in the home country
rather than in the country where the income was earned. Studies have
found that American firms do raise their debt to asset ratios in high
tax jurisdictions.

Some high-tax countries try to thwart this strategy by imposing a
"thin capitalization" rule. For example in Canada if the debt-equity
ratio of a Canadian subsidiary exceeds two to one, the "excessive"
interest expense is not deductible.[5] These laws give the firm a tax
incentive to push debt financing up to the limit. Desai, Foley, and
Hines (2004) find that in practice companies raise debt-to-asset ratios
significantly in higher tax countries.

12.5.3 Tax Havens

Tax Havens are countries that offer themselves to foreign investors as
places with very low income taxes. They also tend to offer high secrecy
from foreign governments. In addition, they claim to offer advanced
communication infrastructure so as to make them suitable places for

---

[5] Canada tightened this rule in 2001. Previously, interest expenses had been deductible up to a debt-equity ratio of 3:1.

financial activity. The majority of countries deemed tax havens are very small and known as "dots." The Cayman Islands is a well-known example. There are just seven tax havens with populations over a million. The "Big 7" tax havens are Hong Kong, Ireland, Lebanon, Liberia, Panama, Singapore, and Switzerland.[6]

It is worth remembering that *under the simple FTC system* described in section 12.2, firms based in a higher tax country end up paying their home-country tax rather than the tax in the haven. There are also limitations to the use of tax havens for MNCs based in exemption-system countries. Governments that offer the exemption system usually do not sign tax treaties with the countries they deem to be tax havens. For example, Canada does not have a tax treaty with Hong Kong or most of the Caribbean island havens and it is only in the negotiation process with Singapore. When governments of developed countries discover loopholes by which a tax haven can be used, they typically change the rules to shut the loophole down. Canada has recently introduced a general anti-avoidance rule, designed to reverse any abusive tax manoeuvre.

Despite these limitations, a recent study by Jim Hines (2004) found that many tax havens are "flourishing." How can that be? For one thing, tax havens can be used illegally. Some entities, particularly those with illegally obtained income, invest in tax havens and simply fail to report their interest income to the home-country tax authorities. That would be a criminal offence which could result in jail time if successfully prosecuted. This is probably why tax havens are known for high secrecy, as well as low taxes.

Tax havens can be used legally as well. As we discussed in section 12.3, FTC systems allowing for payment delay and foreign tax averaging allow the MNC to benefit from shifting income to low-tax jurisdictions. Countries with exemption systems may avoid treaties with most tax havens but not with all of them. Thus, Canada has treaties with Ireland, Switzerland, and Barbados.[7]

Recall that the key to obtaining an exemption or delaying tax under an FTC system is that the subsidiary income must be from an "active business." In other words, if you simply park passive assets in Barbados, the income they generate will be taxed at the same rates as they would

---

[6] This subsection draws heavily on information found in Hines (2004).

[7] A full list of Canada's tax treaties can be found at http://www.fin.gc.ca/treaties/treatystatus_e.html. The corresponding list for the US is contained in http://www.irs.gov/pub/irs-pdf/p901.pdf.

have been at home (assuming you report them). The question then is what type of active business is suitable for the tax haven.

Companies have successfully and legally used tax havens to set up offshore financing companies, captive insurance companies, and central purchasing houses. These activities share certain common features. First, these subsidiaries earn revenues that show up as expenses for other subsidiaries of the MNC. These expenses would be interest, insurance premiums, or material purchases. This shifts income out of the firm's subsidiaries in high-tax areas and over to the tax haven. Later it can be repatriated to the headquarters. The second feature of these activities is that they are services which can be conducted by a relatively small staff. All they need is some office space and good communication infrastructure. This is important since we have seen that most tax havens are small markets and few of them are attractive as export platforms for manufactured goods (Ireland being a prominent exception to this rule). Furthermore tax havens are often rather remote from the MNCs main operations. The services described above can be provided over long distances at relatively low trade costs. Thus we can see these uses of tax havens as fitting within a Vertical Specialization strategy, where the host country has sufficiently high "tax advantages" to compensate for its lack of outstanding factor advantages.

References

Desai, Mihir A., C. Fritz Foley and James R. Hines, Jr., 2004, "A Multinational Perspective On Capital Structure Choice And Internal Capital Markets," *Journal of Finance* 59(6), 2451–2487.

Hines, James R. Jr., 2004, "Do Tax Havens Flourish?" NBER Working Paper No. 10936

13

Expatriate Assignment

Who should the MNE employ to manage its foreign subsidiaries? This is a key question of International human resources management. We will refer to three kinds of employees at foreign locations:

1. Locals: host country nationals,
2. Home country nationals: Citizens of the headquarters country.
3. Third country nationals: individuals from neither the host country nor the headquarters country.

Individuals in categories 2 or 3 are *expatriates*. They are individuals who are on assignment outside their own country.

13.1 Typical Features of Expatriate Assignments

Many readers of this book will have the opportunity to work on overseas assignment for a multinational enterprise. This section provides an idea of what to expect.

13.1.1 Compensation

Persons sent on a temporary foreign assignment (e.g. a few years) are usually paid based on the pay scale of their home country. Often, employers will pay premiums to individuals going on international assignment. In some firms, these premiums may be negotiated on a case by case basis. However, large multi-national employers typically have an established policy that fixes the premium based on which country the employee is in (e.g. 10% of base salary for Australia, 30% for China, 0% for the US, etc.).

There is usually some adjustment for cost of living differences. Housing in foreign locations is often more expensive than at home. Examples of expensive foreign assignment locations include Hong Kong, London, Paris, Singapore, and Tokyo. Normally, employers will therefore compensate employees for the difference in costs. For example, a reasonably spacious apartment in Tokyo might cost $65,000 per year, while normal housing in the home country might cost $10,000. So the employer might cover the full cost of the Tokyo apartment, but deduct $10,000 for hypothetical housing costs from the employee's pay. The net effect is that the employee is not out-of-pocket with respect to housing costs; he or she only bears the cost of normal housing in the home country. Costs of day-to-day living (e.g. food, gas, clothing, consumer goods, automobiles) may also be more expensive in some foreign locations. Many employers provide an additional allowance for these cost-of-living differences.

Taxes often increase as a result of foreign assignments. There are a number of reasons this can happen:

1. Many of the additional compensation items (e.g. premiums, housing, cost-of-living allowances) are taxable. For example, in the Tokyo apartment example above, there would be a $55,000 benefit, which would be taxable in most countries. (The $55,000 is the net cost paid by the employer for housing: the $65,000 rental expense minus the $10,000 recovered from the employee.) If the employee had to bear the cost of the taxes on that benefit, he or she would be out-of-pocket. Accordingly, most employers will therefore pay the taxes arising from such benefits.

2. If an employer pays part of the employee's taxes, that payment is itself a taxable benefit. Suppose for example the marginal tax rate were 45%. Then the employer's total cost of the housing benefit plus the payments required for taxes amount to $100,000 [$55,000 housing cost plus $24,750 taxes on the housing cost plus $20,250 taxes on tax payments]. [The total cost (TC) can be computed directly as TC × (100%-45%) = $55,000.]

3. Foreign taxes may be higher than home country taxes. (This rarely applies to Canadians going overseas because Canada's taxes are high. However, this often applies to American expatriates, because US taxes are relatively low.)

When an employer bears the cost of any additional taxes arising from a foreign assignment, it is called *tax protection*. Many multi-national employers will go a step further and actually recover any tax savings that might be realized from a foreign assignment. For example, if a

Canadian is sent to Hong Kong, his/her legal tax liability will typically be reduced. However, the company will not allow the employee to keep the savings. The company will pay foreign taxes on behalf of the employee, but deduct hypothetical Canadian taxes from the individual's pay. This practice is called *tax equalization*.

Employers often provide time for and cover the cost of visiting home once or twice a year. The costs of moving are also generally covered.

13.1.2 Expatriate Life

Usually foreign operations are smaller than those at home. As a result, expatriates often get a greater breadth of experience overseas. For example, an employee that is in middle management in a large home country operation will often take on a senior position in the smaller foreign operation. The technology in foreign locations might be behind what is available at home. It is often more difficult to get external servicing for leading-edge technology in these locations. Moreover, the large home operation will normally have greater internal support functions and networks, whereas such support may be lacking in smaller overseas operations.

In many organizations, foreign assignments are considered an important part of career development. Individuals aspiring to senior management positions in a multinational company may need to get foreign experience. However, there are some risks associated with foreign assignment. There is the "out of sight, out of mind" problem. There is a tendency for people in foreign locations to be overlooked when decisions concerning career development are made. Yet, an expatriate can adopt strategies to minimize this problem, such as keeping in touch with HQ, visiting the home office whenever he or she is on home leave, and maximizing face time with key decision-makers. The employee may be unaware of opportunities that arise at HQ. An expatriate can minimize this problem by getting a friend at HQ to keep him/her posted on such opportunities.

A foreign assignment can be hard on families. If the individual's spouse has employment, the spouse may have to try to coordinate a transfer to the foreign location, or may have to give up working for the duration of the assignment. Sometimes the spouse will not want to go. Separation from family and friends, and from the amenities at home can be hard. The hardship and loneliness is magnified if the spouse is not occupied with employment at the foreign location.

The foreign assignment can also be difficult for those with children. Such employees often need to decide whether to pull their children away from their current schools and peers, or to be separated from their children for long periods of time. (If the children go on the foreign assignment, there will usually be private international or American schools in the foreign location. Employers will usually cover schooling costs for the children.)

13.2 Selection of Managers in Foreign Locations

One important decision facing multinational enterprises is whom to appoint to senior positions in foreign locations. Is it better to send people from headquarters or to appoint locals?

13.2.1 Advantages of Expats

1. Expertise in the firm-specific advantages of the MNE. Expatriates reassigned from HQ are familiar with the company's products, core competencies, global operations, systems, industry and senior managers.
2. Awareness of activities of MNE in other countries and, consequently, the ability to coordinate them effectively.
3. Larger pool of talented managers to draw from. In some countries, competent managers with experience in the firm's industry may be in short supply.
4. Expatriates tend to be more well-known and trusted at headquarters, because they have spent time with personnel at HQ. This facilitates getting appropriate resources from HQ, and helps HQ to take more seriously what they are being told about what is happening in the foreign location.
5. A multinational firm may be able to use foreign operations as testing-grounds or a place of learning for potential senior managers.

13.2.2 Advantages of Locals

1. Local managers speak the local language.
2. Local managers are aware of (and usually follow) local customs in how to do business.
3. Local managers are more likely to understand the needs, expectations and practices of local customers.
4. Locals have local relationships with important customers (or intermediaries like wholesalers and retailers).

5. Locals are more likely to have contacts within government and the regulatory commissions.
6. Local managers are usually better regarded by the public. They do not engender as much resentment for being over-paid and pampered.
7. Local managers are almost always cheaper than expatriates.
   a) Additional training (language, culture).
   b) Immigration authorization hassles.
   c) Compensation for higher cost of living or "hardship" or higher taxes.
8. Expats have high *failure rates*: Difficulties in adjustment to the new environment by either the manager or her spouse may result in early return to the home country. This means the MNE has wasted the investment in training and immigration authorization.
9. Having locals in senior management also helps the company to attract and retain good employees, since there is a visible upward career track.

13.2.3 Strategy and Staffing

Which MNE strategy favours which staffing approach? The replication strategy puts an emphasis on local manufacturing and marketing and thus will particularly benefit from the host-country manager's local expertise and connections. Meanwhile the lack of awareness of the rest of the MNE's activities will not be too harmful because MNEs pursuing replication strategies do little coordination across geographical divisions.

Many companies use the following procedure: When starting up at a foreign location, use expatriate managers who are familiar with the company's products and systems. The expatriates facilitate the transfer of the firm's key advantages (or core competencies) to the new subsidiary. Each expatriate will usually have a host-country national as an "apprentice" (but also as a source of local expertise). Then promote local people to management positions, once they have acquired familiarity with the company's products and systems. Gradually the expatriates will be removed and their apprentices will take their positions.

Some companies take a "global" approach to management, and move managers (of all nationalities) around from location to location. The objective is to have managers all over the world who are familiar with the operations of other parts of the world. These two methods can be combined. The idea is that the firm should economize on the small number of key managers who can transmit corporate culture and capabilities to overseas affiliates. These people will be not only good at their jobs but also comfortable with life in new foreign environments. After they have trained local replacements, they move on to the next recently established or restructured affiliate.

Printing: Krips bv, Meppel
Binding: Stürtz, Würzburg